Flower Arranging

JUDITH BLACKLOCK

teach
yourself®

For UK order enquiries: please contact Bookpoint Ltd, 130 Milton Park, Abingdon, Oxon OX14 4SB. Telephone: (44) 01235 827720. Fax: (44) 01235 400454. Lines are open from 09.00–18.00, Monday to Saturday, with a 24-hour message answering service. You can also order through our website www.madaboutbooks.com

For USA order enquiries: please contact McGraw-Hill Customer Services, P.O. Box 545, Blacklick, OH 43004-0545, USA. Telephone: 1-800-722-4726. Fax: 1-614-755-5645.

For Canada order enquiries: please contact McGraw-Hill Ryerson Ltd, 300 Water St, Whitby, Ontario L1N 9B6, Canada. Telephone: 905 430 5000. Fax: 905 430 5020.

Long-renowned as the authoritative source for self-guided learning – with more than 30 million copies sold worldwide – the *Teach Yourself* series includes over 300 titles in the fields of languages, crafts, hobbies, business and education.

British Library Cataloguing in Publication Data
A catalogue record for this title is available from The British Library.

Library of Congress Catalog Card Number: On file.

First published in UK 2001 by Hodder Headline Ltd, 338 Euston Road, London NW1 3BH

First published in US 2001 by Contemporary Books, a Division of The McGraw-Hill Companies, 1 Prudential Plaza, 130 East Randolph Street, Chicago, Illinois 60601 USA.

The 'Teach Yourself' name is a registered trade mark of Hodder & Stoughton Ltd.

Cover photo from Steve Tanner
Typeset by Dorchester Typesetting Group Ltd, Dorchester, Dorset.
Printed in Dubai for Hodder & Stoughton Educational, a division of Hodder Headline Plc., 338 Euston Road, London NW1 3BH.

Impression number 10 9 8 7 6 5 4 3 2 1
Year   2009 2008 2007 2006 2005 2004 2003

Contents

Acknowledgements

I would like to thank students and friends who have contributed arrangements for the book, in particular Carla Barbaglia, Christina Curtis and Ann-Marie Kendrick. I would also like to thank Dr. Curtis for her careful botanical work on plant names, and Ron for being the ever-willing chauffeur.

Special mention must be given to the NAFAS and IEFA teachers whom I met in Dromentine, Northern Ireland who encouraged me to include all the classic designs from my first edition of *Teach Yourself Flower Arranging*. Hannelore Billat-Reinhardt was also at Dromentine and she generously gave advice on the characteristics of contemporary design. Deborah Hutton provided me with details of WAFA and we both hope that this information will draw new members into this exciting worldwide movement. I much appreciate all of their help and support.

My husband David, children Charles and Jane, and mother Joan Ward deserve special mention for all their help and cooperation since the time long ago when flower arranging took over my life!

Arrangement acknowledgements

The flower designers whose work appears in this book are:

Ann-Marie Kendrick (pages 15, 76, 90)
Helena Harris (page 16)
Andreas Verheyen (pages 20, 95)
Ann Diebel (page 26)
Ashley Casson (page 32)
Dr Christina Curtis (pages 40, 70, 92, 96, 98)
Stephen Collier (page 46)
Sue Davis (page 61)

Shän Roscoe (page 87)
Per Benjamin (pages 91, 100)
Chris Jones (page 94)
Manfred Hoffman (page 97)
Leon for the Flower Council of Holland (page 99)
Carla Barbaglia (pages 106–107)

Photo acknowledgements

The author and publishers would like to thank the following for their kind permission to reproduce photographs:

Steve Tanner (front cover, pages 6, 7)

Mike Pannett (pages 9, 10, 13, 19, 25, 26, 27, 28, 32, 33, 34, 36, 40, 41, 42, 43, 44, 45, 47, 53, 54, 57, 58, 59, 61, 70, 73, 76, 80, 87, 88, 90, 92, 96, 98, 101, 102–103, 111, 112, 113)

Flower and Plants Association (page 77)

International Flower Bulb Bureau (page 97)

Rosolani (pages 107–108)

Introduction

Flower Arranging, floral art, flower design – are they one and the same? The expression 'flower arranging' seems dated but in fact there is nothing to distinguish it from the more contemporary expression 'floral design'.

Flower arranging was once the domain of the lady at home – the amateur who enjoyed the art of placing flowers in the vase, doing the church flowers, entering competitions and visiting flower clubs for information and a social occasion. The garden was an important source of plant material.

Floristry was and is the world of the professional who works with flowers as a creative trade.

Over the past ten years the world of the flower arranger and the florist have moved closer together. Flower arrangers now take advantage of the vast range of flowers and exotic foliage that can be obtained over the counter. Many supplement the family income by working from home. The professional floristry world is peopled by those who work in shops, supermarkets and from flower stalls. There are many full-time contractors who work from home. Garden foliage is now available at the flower markets and the increasing use of foliage in florists' designs makes the distinction between the two worlds more difficult to recognize.

The increased availability of containers in ceramics, metal, basketry and wood and the many new varieties of plant material from all corners of the world makes the world of flowers today exciting, innovative and forward thinking.

The surge in modern technology has made communication easy and international trends and techniques have influenced the world of flowers. There is now an exciting worldwide flower movement. Many countries belong to the Association entitled WAFA (Worldwide Association of Floral Arrangers) – see pages 114–115 for further information.

It is hard to say who leads the world in flower arranging. Style frequently arises from a crossover of ideas and techniques. There is always inspiration to be found from anyone working in or who is passionate about the world of flowers.

Everything you need to know about the background to flower arranging can be found in Chapters 1–4. Chapter 5 covers classical flower design and Chapter 6 covers contemporary flower design. Step-by-step techniques are covered in depth in the classical section, as this is the ideal starting point for flower arrangers. Once you learn the elements and principles of flower arranging you will be able to create any design that you wish.

And if you want to learn more, interior and fashion magazines are ideal for finding out about current trends and colours. Many hotels display flowers and it is easy to wander into the lobby to view the displays. Visiting flower shops and flower stalls is a good way of discovering new and different varieties of plant material. Trends in containers can be viewed at stores. Even the supermarkets are worth visiting for inspiration.

Judith Blacklock

Choosing your plant material

The key to successful flower arranging is to get the right combination of plant material together before you start. For most designs you will need flowers and foliage. They may be grown and picked from the garden or purchased at the flower shop, the supermarket, market stall or flower market.

If you are purchasing your flowers it is best to purchase from one or a couple of sources on a regular basis then you will be assured of getting good service and quality plant material.

Points to observe when purchasing flowers and foliage

■ Leaves on the flowers should be a healthy green and not yellow.
■ There should be no leaves on the stems below the water level.
■ The florets that make up the yellow disc at the centre of spray chrysanthemums should not have released their pollen.
■ When purchasing spray chrysanthemums, or other flowers with secondary stems, for use in small arrangements, long secondary stems will mean you can use them individually.

■ Spray chrysanthemums with varying lengths of secondary stems. The stem on the left is easier to use.

Some flowers have a longer life than others – do not expect *Iris* to last as long as carnations.

When buying mixed foliage choose one variety with a smooth texture, such as *Eucalyptus*.

Lilies and *Freesia* should have plump buds and have one flower open or on the point of opening.

The stem ends should not be discoloured and look cooked. This can be due to the stems having been conditioned in water that was too hot. This consequently affects the life span of the stem.

There should be no loose pollen on the petals as this indicates the flowers are nearing the end of their life.

Most flowers should be displayed inside the shop as they are vulnerable to drafts.

Double flowers usually last longer than single flowers.

Conditioning plant material

If you give time and thought to arranging flowers attractively it is important that the flowers do not wilt or die before the end of their natural cut life. The process by which this is done is called conditioning.

Plant material dies prematurely if bacteria enters the stem. Bacteria are produced in dirty water, dirty buckets, dirty containers and on dirty scissors, knives and secateurs. It is therefore of utmost importance that all your components and implements are spotlessly clean so that your plant material can last the maximum length of time.

Plant material from the florist has usually been well conditioned but the same simple procedure given below is advisable once stem ends have been out of water.

To condition plant material

1 The bottom few centimetres should be removed on the slant with a sharp clean pair of florists' scissors. (Florists will usually use a sharp knife but for many this is more difficult to use). This diagonal cut exposes the largest amount of inner tissue and it is this tissue which contains the vessels taking water up to the flowers and leaves. It also prevents a stem end forming a seal against the container.

2 Cut just above the node (the nobbly bits that occur at regular intervals on the stem). Cutting just below or on the nodes impedes the uptake of water.

3 Remove any leaves which would go below the water line as long term submersion causes decomposition and the spread of bacteria.

4 The cut stem ends should be placed immediately in a bucket or container of deep, warm water and left in a cool place for a couple of hours. A warm liquid travels more quickly than a cool one because it has less air in it. The two exceptions to this rule are when using chrysanthemums and *Bouvardia* which need cool water. The water should be deep because a certain amount of water can also enter the plant through the surface of the stem.

5 The plant material should be left in a cool place because more water evaporates through the pores on the leaves when the atmosphere is warmer or drier. This is also why arrangements should be placed away from draughts, central heating and the heat given out by televisions. The water is needed in the stem, not in the atmosphere.

6 All bulb flowers should have their whitish stem ends cut off. Bulb flowers last longer in shallow rather than deep water. Their stems generally are softer and thicker than other flowers and are therefore easier to place on a pinholder than in foam. Daffodils secrete a sticky sap, which is poisonous to other flowers. However, if daffodils are left on their own in water for 24 hours they can then be arranged with other flowers. Wipe the stem ends gently but do not recut them.

7 Collect flowers and foliage from the garden in the evening, if possible. By this time the maximum reserves of food will be stored in the plant to be used during the hours of darkness. The cool of evening also means that little moisture is being lost through the leaves by transpiration.

8 The stem of certain plant material, such as plants in the spurge family (*Euphorbiaceae*), contains a milky sap

called latex. This sap is an irritant and care must be taken not to touch the eyes after handling. Once cut, hold the stem end in a flame to prevent the sap oozing out and blocking the stem entrance. If this procedure is not followed water cannot enter the stem.

9 If your garden foliage grows in an urban area, wash away dirt by submerging in water to which a drop of washing-up liquid has been added. Immature foliage can get waterlogged if you leave it too long but you can leave more mature foliage for up to an hour. Rinse the foliage well before using. Silver or grey foliage should not be submerged.

Tips and treatments

Flowers from the florist have frequently been treated with a silver nitrate solution which retards the ageing process. This is why flowers such as sweet peas, purchased from a florist, can now last more than five days. It is ethylene gas that shortens the life of cut plant material. Unfortunately ethylene is given off by numerous forms of life, in particular ripening fruit and vegetables and decaying plant material. So you should always remove the dying heads on a flower spray and keep flowers which are particularly susceptible, such as carnations, *Gypsophila* and orchids, away from fruit and vegetables.

Tips and treatments that work

Cut flower food
The sachets of cut flower food that are given with flowers from many florists and supermarkets do enable your plant material to last longer. The special formula prevents the rapid increase of bacteria and helps the flowers and foliage to develop to their full potential. The water should **not** be changed, only added to. There are special formulae for specific flowers such as cut shrub and tree stems and bulb flowers.

Aspirin
The latest scientific research seems to show that aspirin helps stimulate a plant's defence mechanism so adding a small amount of aspirin to the water may indeed help to defend the plant against bacteria.

The dishwasher
The dishwasher makes your containers spotlessly clean but take care that you do not use one to wash containers made from glass composed of various thicknesses as these will crack under the heat.

Tips and treatments that do not work

Sugar or lemonade
Sugar and the sugar in lemonade is a food for bacteria as well as the flowers and as a consequence bacteria will multiply if this is added to the water.

Smashing and hammering the stems
Do not hammer or smash the stem ends. Research shows that this only causes harm. The ensuing damage to cell tissue encourages the rapid growth of bacteria and thus reduces the life of the plant material. If you are removing thorns from roses great care should be taken that the stem is not damaged thus allowing bacteria to enter. The thorns should only be removed immediately prior to use in an arrangement.

2

Getting started – flowers in containers

N o equipment is essential to get you going, except for a vase or container. The term 'vase' usually means a vessel of traditional form and material whereas the word 'container' embraces both the traditional and the contemporary. The term container will be used for this reason.

This chapter explains how you can effectively arrange flowers in a container and describe the technique for a handtied bouquet. Learning this technique will enthuse, give confidence and lead you on to understanding the techniques and equipment for other designs explained in later chapters.

Choosing the plant material

If you follow the guidelines below your flowers will always look successful:

- If using a mass of flowers and foliage the volume of the plant material should be one and a half times the volume of the container. Alternatively, the container can be one and a half times the volume

■ Left: The plant material of *Anemone* and *Eucalyptus* dominates the grey and cream pottery container.

■ The container has more importance than the plant material of *Hypericum* 'Excellent' berries and *Rosa* 'Naranga'.

■ Mauve-pink roses and bright orange *Dianthus* (carnations) combine harmoniously through the addition of dark green ivy which surrounds and links these two colours.

of the flowers. What should be avoided is the flowers and the vase being of equal volume. One needs to dominate the other in order to give visual harmony.

■ A mass of one type of flower always looks good. You can arrange one variety together in varying hues – from one end of the spectrum to the other. They will always look good if the container and the flowers are in proportion and in harmony.

■ If mixing your flowers always include at least one variety which has a round face such as gerberas, carnations or marigolds.

■ The addition of green foliage works as it is a harmonizer of all the other elements in the design whatever colour combination you have chosen.

■ If you have only a few flowers for your container they need a strong form. As the volume will be less than stated previously they need to be on longer stems, as the space between the stems will become part of the overall proportion. They could be two to three times the height of the container to compensate for the lack of mass.

■ Reflect the colour of your vase in the flowers used. Copper is good with pinks, peaches, mauves, apricots

Choosing containers

If you are choosing a container and are overwhelmed by the range and diversity of those on offer you would be safe to select:

■ two or three straight-sided glass containers of various sizes, square or round;
■ a plain, sculptural vase in a classic, undemanding colour and texture, approximately 18 cm (7.5 in) in height.

■ The rusty brown tones of the container link with the warm-orange of the candle and roses. Sympathetic contrast is given by the green *Skimmia japonica* and the longer stems of the pussy willow.

and reds. Brass suits creams, yellows, oranges, greens and browns. Silver, alabaster and pewter are lovely with creams, white, pinks, blues and greys.
■ Bear grass or steel grass gives movement and interest to all designs. It is long lasting and stylish.

■ *Dianthus barbatus* (sweet William) and *Skimmia* have been placed in a jam jar within a square glass tank. The area between the jam jar and the glass tank has been lined with lengths of lipstick bamboo (see overleaf).

Handtieds

A handtied is a bunch of flowers and foliage which has been arranged in the hand and tied, ready to be placed in a container. It can be wrapped in its own aquapack to give as the perfect gift. Once you have got the knack you will find that arranging your own handtied is the perfect relaxation. Most people need about five attempts to get the knack of creating the spiral and then they never look back!

You will need:

20–40 stems of flowers and foliage. When selecting your plant material consider the following:

- Choose at least one variety of flowers with a round open face.
- Spray flowers, berries and foliage pack out a handtied and help to separate feature flowers.
- Avoid flowers which are in tight bud because you will want immediate impact.
- Avoid flowers with soft stems such as daffodils and anemones because they may be squashed when tied.
- Choose flowers with approximately the same lifespan.
- Avoid stems which branch low down such as spray carnations.
- Avoid stems which are very thick. Thin stems are easier to hold.
- Flowers with great variance in their stem length can be awkward to handle together.
- Smooth, round thick stems are difficult to hold – they tend to slip as you cross one over the other.

Despite the seemingly long list of do's and don'ts the handtied is easy to master. You will also need some garden twine and sharp scissors or secateurs.

Creating the design

1 Pre-cut a length of twine about 45 cm (18 in) long.
2 Remove all leaves from the lower two thirds of each stem. All exposed stems must be immaculately clean. Thorns should be carefully removed from roses.
3 Place your flowers and foliage in groups on a clean uncluttered surface.
4 Have your twine and scissors close to hand.
5 Bend your left arm (right-handed people) or right arm (left-handed people) so that your hand is flat in front of you. Close the fingers firmly, leaving the thumb flexible so that stems can be placed between the thumb and the palm of the hand.
6 You must now build your spiral of flowers. This means your stems will be angled in the same direction round a central pivot. This is achieved by:
   (a) Inserting a central vertical stem between the palm of your hand and your thumb
   (b) Angling a second stem across the first, just under the flowers or foliage so that you are gripping clean stems. This stem must cross the first stem cleanly and obviously. It must not simply lie parallel with the first stem, it must cross.
   (c) Placing a third stem at a sharper angle to the second stem and repeating this action with further stems.

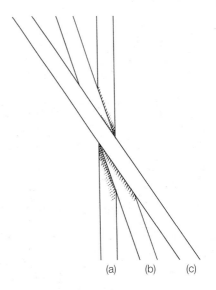

(a)   (b)   (c)

■ Angling the first three stems.

7 When all your stems have been included, wrap the garden twine round the stems at the point at which they cross over each other. Tie as high as you can on the bare stems. Avoid tying over any leaves at the top of the stems.

8 Cut the stems to the same length. The width of the handtied should be approximately one and a half times the height. This will give good proportions.

9 Tap the stem ends on a hard surface so that the bouquet will stand.

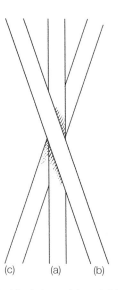

■ Tucking stem (c) behind stems (a) and (b).

■ A simple handtied bouquet of roses, herbs and *Gaultheria shallon* (salal) and *Mentha* foliage.

(d) At this point you may wish to add flowers to the rear of the design. To do this relax your hand and tuck a stem behind so that the flowers circle round in the same direction (see above right).

(e) Build up the spiral by placing all your stems one over the other with the occasional stem behind to get good balance of plant material. You will be able to significantly relax your hand now so that the heads of the plant material move closer together and your handtied gains structure and substance.

Adding a foliage surround

Long lasting, strong green leaves can create a simple but effective 'frill' around your handtied. *Aspidistra*, croton or small palm leaves are ideal. If you are using the longer *Aspidistra* or croton leaves simply bring the point of the leaf down to the top of the stem and with a length of florists' tape 'wrap' the two together. You will need 5–7 stems depending on the size of your bouquet. Add these to the handtied. You may prefer to tie your handtied then add your frill of leaves and tie again.

■ A plastic bottle has been cut down, filled with water and decorated with long-lasting *Magnolia* leaves and a twist of ivy. A handtied of mimosa and tulips have been placed in the container.

■ Adding water to a handtied aquapack.

Handtied aquapack

As we have discussed, stem ends form a seal immediately they have been taken from a water source. Creating an aquapack is the ideal way to transport your flowers so that the recipient needs only place the gift on the side and transfer the flowers to a vase at his/her convenience.

Creating an aquapack

1   Pre-cut a length of garden twine. Cut a square of cellophane. Place the handtied centrally on the cellophane and ensure it keeps firm contact with the stem ends. If the stems are widely splayed out tighten your hold so they come closer together.

2   Draw the four corners of the cellophane up around the flowers and draw them in at the tying point of your handtied. Allow no excess air to enter which will create air pockets. Tie with your string. Add ribbon or raffia to finish. Take a jug of water and pour water gently through the centre of the handtied.

Incorporating fabric

Semi-opaque fabric can also be incorporated into the design to give a new and different look. Take a square of fabric and cut a small hole in the centre through which the stems of your handtied will pass. Point the handtied downwards so that the material flows away from the stems. Add more stems outside the fabric (this is easier than it sounds). Return the handtied to the upward position and bring the fabric into the binding point. Tie with wire-edged ribbon.

■ Semi-opaque fabric and flowers – ideal for a wedding bouquet. A mass of cream 'Bianca' and 'Tineke' roses surrounded by soft flowing fabric.

■ Left: This handtied bouquet of *Helianthus annuus* (sunflowers), *Leucospermum cordifolium* (pincushion protea), *Leucadendron* 'Safari Sunset', *Rosa* 'Grand Prix', *Berzelia squarrosa* (green protea), and *Dracaena reflexa* 'Song of India' is finished with looped leaves of *Aspidistra elatior*. Coconut fibre has been wrapped around a simple glass vase and the handtied bouquet simply inserted inside.

3

Mechanics and sundries

Mechanics

Mechanics is the word used for all equipment that will keep your stems in place. Floral foam, chicken wire and a pinholder are those used traditionally but with changes in the floral scene, twigs, test tubes, gravel, and shells are all used to give greater diversity of design.

Floral foam

Floral foam was invented by a chemist called Vernon Smithers in the early 1940s, quite by mistake. It is light, easily available and is made of resins which restrict the growth of bacteria so that the flowers last longer. For flower arrangers the greatest advantage that foam gives is that it enables stems to be inserted at all angles so that plant material can give graceful flow to a design. For traditional designs the foam should therefore rise at least 2.5 cm (1 in) above the rim for smaller arrangements and 5 cm (2 in) for larger arrangements. Pare a little foam off the sharp angles, *very* gently, to soften the shape. This is called *chamfering*.

■ Chicken wire secured around a plastic bowl and covered with boxwood is filled with fragrant garden roses, *Origanum* sp. flowers, *Lavendula* sp. flowers, *Mentha* sp., *Pelargonium* sp. (scented geranium) and variegated ivy.

The most commonly-known brand is perhaps Oasis. It can be purchased in different sizes – jumbo blocks, designer sheets, cylinders, balls, and cones but usually in bricks. The green foam is soaked and used for fresh stems. The grey foam will not absorb water and is used for dried and silk flowers.

Do not use too large a piece of foam. The more you use, the more you will have to hide.

How to soak your foam
A brick of Oasis can absorb water in under a minute. To soak foam so that it absorbs water throughout fill a basin or bowl with water that is deeper and wider than the piece you wish to soak. To prevent dry areas occurring in the foam you should gently lower the foam horizontally onto the surface of the water. It will sink under its own weight until foam appears just above the level of the water and bubbles cease forming around the block. This will take approximately 60 seconds. Do not oversoak or the foam tends to crumble when you insert many stems.

If after use your foam is intact with only a few stem holes, it may be kept by placing the foam in a plastic bag which is firmly tied. Once used foam must not be allowed to dry out. If it does dry out boiling water to which a drop of washing-up liquid has been added should be poured over the foam. It can then be reused but it will not retain water as efficiently as the fresh.

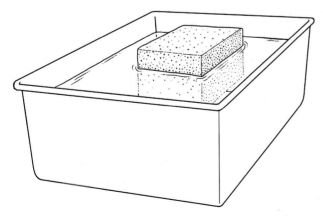

■ Wetting a piece of foam.

Chicken wire

Chicken wire can be purchased from ironmongers or DIY stores in different mesh sizes and will be galvanised. If purchased from a florists' wholesalers you will have the opportunity of buying green plastic-coated wire which although more expensive is gentler on the hands. Chicken wire can be used in the following ways.

Around a container
A long length of small gauge chicken wire can be folded in three and secured around the perimeter of a basket. If a small hole is pierced through opposite sides of the plastic bowl and a length of reel wire is taken over the chicken wire will stay securely in place. Lengths of box or other long lasting foliage can then be inserted through the chicken wire (see page 16).

Inside the container
This is the ideal method for securing the stems of soft stems and for flowers which need loads of water such as spring flowers, anemones etc.

A good mesh size for this purpose is the 5 cm (2 in). The amount you use depends to some extent on the size of the container and the thickness of the stems you wish to insert. A rough guideline would be to cut a piece a little wider than the width of the opening and about three times the depth. Cut off the selvedge as this is stiff. Crumple the netting so that it forms approximately the same shape as the container.

Fill the container with water and thread your stems through the chicken wire. If the mesh of your wire is small the holes will disappear to nothing once you have several layers.

If you need extra support, particularly if you are using thick-stemmed heavy branches, place a pinholder in the bottom of your container. Allow your first placement through the chicken wire to be well impaled on the pinholder and this will secure the netting firmly.

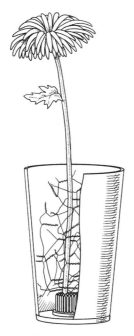

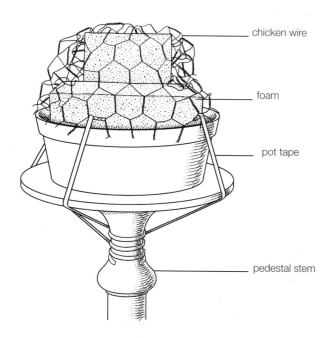

■ Chicken wire as a mechanic with a pinholder at the base of the container to give added support.

chicken wire

foam

pot tape

pedestal stem

■ Mechanics for a pedestal design.

Around foam

When creating a large scale arrangement you will be using heavy stems which may need extra support. A cap of small gauge chicken wire placed gently over the foam and secured with wire will give strength to your mechanics. Chicken wire with a 1.25 cm (0.5 in) gauge is suitable for this purpose. The larger 5 cm (2 in) chicken wire cuts into the foam too deeply.

Pinholder

Pinholders come in many shapes and sizes. Only one pinholder is necessary for beginners and indeed for many more advanced arrangers. The most useful size is probably 6.25 cm (2.5 in) in diameter but a 5 cm (2 in) or 7.5 cm (3 in) would be fine.

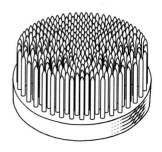

A good pinholder should have:

■ brass pins rather than those made from steel. Brass pins are yellow, steel are grey. Brass pins do not rust, steel pins do;
■ a lead base that is heavy in the hand;
■ pins that are close together and firmly embedded in the lead.

Avoid placing foam directly onto a pinholder. It is extremely difficult to remove all traces later unless you place a piece of nylon tights onto the pins first.

Plant material with hard stems should have its stem end cut at a sharp angle before being eased between or onto the pins. It can then be angled using gentle pressure. Be careful when placing hard materials as the pins are sharp. If a stem refuses to stay in place – and this can happen to even the most accomplished of arrangers – slit the stem upwards. It will then go on the pins more easily and you will not damage the holder. Alternatively, tie 4–5 thinner stems to the outside of a thick, hard stem. The thinner stems

■ A single *Cymbidium* orchid flower, with its stem end in a plastic orchid tube, is supported by twigs cut to the same length.

should protrude beyond the main stem end. String should be used for the tie as it shrinks in water and improves bonding. Thin stems are difficult to use on a pinholder. You can tie several together with wool and this will then slip easily onto a pin. Alternatively place thin stems inside thicker hollow stems to wedge on pins.

The pinholder can be simply placed onto a dish but if you would prefer it to be more secure use Oasis fix to secure it in position.

You can place flat pebbles or moss over your pinholder in order to hide it.

Twigs

Uniform, short lengths of twigs are ideal for hiding and supporting a test tube containing a single flower.

Test tubes

Glass test tubes are of great value to the flower designer. They support a stem neatly and decoratively and can be attached to plant material so that interest can be obtained unobtrusively without a mish-mash of stems. The tubes can be disguised with a long-lasting leaf secured with raffia or decorative wire.

■ This design was created from an intricate structure of tall glass containers, woody structures and test tubes. The glass test tubes are pleasing to view and support and give water to stems of *Gloriosa superba* 'Rothschildiana', *Sandersonia*, *Zantedeschia* var., mixed *Rosa* var. (roses), and *Eustoma grandiflorum* (lisianthus) in unconventional positions.

Sellotape

For glass containers transparent adhesive tape can be criss-crossed over the opening to give support. Once you have positioned the plant material the tape can be covered with moss.

Sundries

The hardware

Sundries describes the aids and accessories that can be used in flower arranging. There are hundreds but I have chosen the ones I consider most useful.

Florists' tape

There are two types of florists' tape. Pot tape and anchor tape. Pot tape breaks quite easily whereas anchor tape has been reinforced with cotton threads and is therefore more suitable for more substantial securing.

The adhesive on these tapes sticks firmly to both wet and dry foam. The ends should be wrapped round the container to keep the foam and container as one. Avoid using too many widths across the foam as this will limit the space for stems.

When creating a symmetrical design use the tape off-centre as the central area will need to be free for the placement of stems.

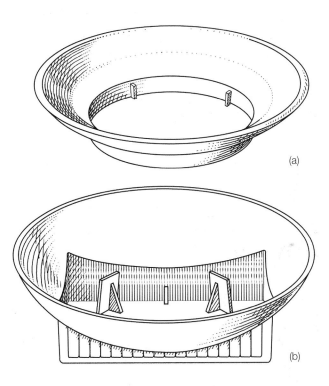

(a)

(b)

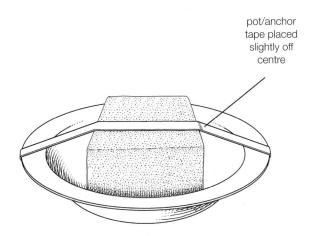

pot/anchor tape placed slightly off centre

■ Anchoring foam.

Green plastic containers

The dishes shown above will enable you to create a wide variety of designs. They are especially useful for table arrangements. Do not worry if you cannot find them at your garden centre – any small, shallow receptacle which retains water will do. Buy the green dishes not the white as the white stands out and distracts from the flowers unless you are going to use a lot of white in your selected colour scheme.

These dishes are useful, however, because:

■ they have been especially designed so that in (a) a cylinder of foam and in (b) a section of a brick of foam will fit snugly and securely

- they are unbreakable
- they are inexpensive so if you are creating flowers for a large function there is no need for the containers to be returned.

Candlecup

Empty bottles and candlesticks are often used as containers for graceful raised arrangements. All you need to adapt them for flower arranging is a candlecup. This is a metal or plastic bowl with a protruding knob to insert in the neck of a bottle or candlestick. They are widely available in white or black but can be easily sprayed any colour to match your container.

If you cannot find a candlecup a cork can be glued to the bottom of a small plastic dish.

To keep the candlecup from wobbling you will need some florists' fix.

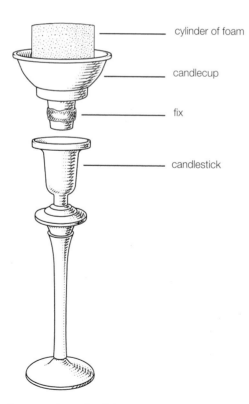

cylinder of foam

candlecup

fix

candlestick

■ A candlecup and candlestick.

Candles

The range of candles available is immense. There is a plastic holder designed to take a slim taper candle but the thicker church-type candle needs to be secured by placing 4–7 short lengths of cocktail/kebab/garden stick on a piece of florists' tape. The tape is then wrapped tightly around the base of the candle. There should only be a small amount of stick above the tape.

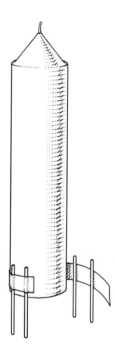

Fix

This is similar to Blu Tack, plasticine or chewing gum and indeed these can be used as an alternative. Fix is used when two hard surfaces need to be held together securely but not permanently. A small piece of fix needs to be worked and warmed in the hands before use to make it more malleable. It can only be used to good effect when the two surfaces to be held together are dry and free of dust. A thin sausage of fix can be wrapped round the protruding knob of the aforementioned candlecup to ensure good contact between the inside of the bottle neck or candlestick hole and the cup.

Fix is difficult to remove because it is sticky so if you are using a silver or brass candlestick protect it by using a strip of Sellotape against the metal. The fix then makes contact with the Sellotape and the candlecup and not the metal and the candlecup. Fix is also used with frogs and pinholders. Residual amounts can be removed with turpentine or white spirit.

Foam Holders

A foam holder or *frog* is a round plastic disc with four prongs. It is used to secure foam to a container which has not been specifically designed to take its shape. A strip of four pea-sized blobs of fix should be pressed on to the dry, dustfree undersurface of the

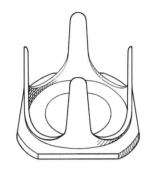

■ A foam holder or frog.

frog at regular intervals. The frog and fix are then placed firmly in position in the container. Your piece of foam is then placed on the prongs of the frog.

Secateurs

These are invaluable for cutting strong and woody stems, especially when cutting the ends of a handtied or branches.

Scissors

Buying a good pair of floral scissors is essential. Household scissors will only frustrate you, squash the stems and perhaps cut your fingers. Your first pair of scissors should have short blades, a serrated inner edge and for preference a notch to allow the easy cutting of thicker stems and wire. They must also be easy to grasp. When buying a pair, check if there is enough room for your fingers and thumb to fit comfortably in the handles.

Wires

Florists' wire is available in a wide range of lengths, weights (gauges) and colours. The purpose of wire is to support, lengthen stems, reduce the weight by replacing the stem and with the addition of coloured wires can also be decorative. The basic guideline is to use the lightest wire possible for your purpose. In the metric system the thicker the wire the higher the number. For the flower arranger new to the art I would suggest that you acquire three thicknesses or gauges of cut wire. A heavy wire of 1.25 mm or 1.00 mm, a medium wire of 0.90 mm and a light wire of 0.56 mm or 0.46 mm.

For wreaths it is also a good idea to obtain binding wire of 0.56 mm thickness.

Reel wire is available in copper, brass, and gold, and metallic red, green and new colours are becoming available.

German pins, rather like open hairpins, are ideal for pinning moss and leaves to foam.

The software

Moss

Moss gives texture, softness and colour and the most commonly used mosses are:

Sphagnum moss retains moisture and is ideal for mossing wreaths and hanging baskets. It is used for these properties rather than for its colour which tends to be on the straw side of green.

Carpet or flat moss is a strong green colour and has a flat earth backing. It is perfect for covering large areas quickly and evenly.

Reindeer moss (Cladonis rangiferina) is a soft spongy moss that has frequently been treated with a softening agent, such as glycerine, to which a dye is often added. Natural and green coloured reindeer moss are recommended for giving wonderful texture and for hiding mechanics.

Bun moss (Leucobryum glaucum) is available in soft gently undulating mounds in the freshest of green.

Tillandsia The natural grey hanging strands of these air plants or Spanish moss are excellent for covering surfaces and adding texture.

Stones and pebbles

The smooth form and texture of stones and pebbles means that they are ideal for incorporating into arrangements. Look at the parallel design on page 88 where stones are used at the base of the design.

Cones

Cones of all sizes and from all conifers are useful to the flower designer.

- To mount small to medium-sized cones wrap a wire round the lowest part of the cone, between the scales, pulling it tight but leaving each end loose. Take the loose ends, bring them both together under the base of the cone and twist to form your stalk.

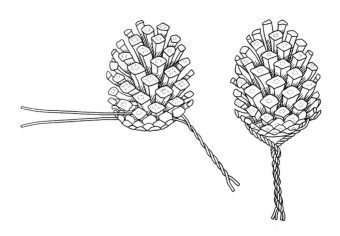

- Wiring method for larger cones.

- Closed cones can have a stick or wire glued to their base.

Raffia

Raffia provides a natural tie that always enhances rather than takes away from the flowers. Neutral and green raffia always work well.

- Wiring method for smaller cones.

- Use two wires to mount larger cones. Hold both wires horizontally, one each side of the cone and force each one as low as possible between the scales. Twist the two ends at each side together. Pull under the base of the cone and twist together to form a stalk.

4

Elements and principles of design

Form, texture, colour and space are the elements of design. You take these elements to create each and every arrangement. As you create there are certain guidelines or principles to follow. These principles are termed balance, scale, proportion, rhythm, contrast and dominance.

If the elements and principles are used well your arrangement will be attractive to the viewer and hold their attention.

The majority of flower arrangements can be termed either mass line or mass. Mass line incorporates space with a denser area of plant material as its focus. A mass arrangement uses plant material without space and the focus is centred on form, colour and texture.

■ A mass arrangement of red roses in a long trough.

■ A mass line arrangement. *Molucella laevis*, myrtle (huckleberry) and *Leucadendron* 'Safari Sunset' provide the line element. *Paeonia* sp. and looped *Cordyline fruticosa* 'Mambo' give mass and focal interest.

Elements of Design
Form

Form is the word used to describe the volumetric
'shape' of a stem of flowers or foliage, i.e. something
three dimensional. 'Shape' is normally used to
describe something two dimensional, or flat, such as
writing on a page.

The form of flowers and stems can be loosely
categorised as being:

- linear
- round
- spray

Linear forms

Linear forms are used to create the shape or form of
the design – its skeleton. This skeleton sets the limits
or boundaries of the arrangement. Linear foliage is
often reinforced by line flowers such as larkspur,
gladioli, *Liatris*, Canterbury bells. When creating the
classic designs linear forms are usually placed in
position first.

■ In this design
Rosmarinus officialis
(rosemary) provides the
linear interest. Yellow
Dianthus (carnations) are
massed to provide contrast
of colour and form.

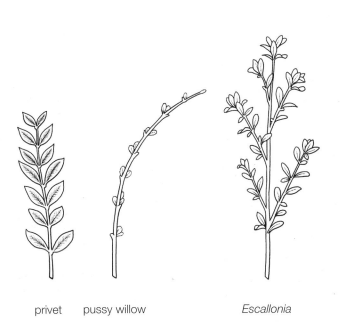

privet   pussy willow   *Escallonia*   *Delphinium*   ■ Line forms.

Round forms

Round, circular forms are the focus of any arrangement. They are the stars of the design as the eye is automatically drawn to their inward moving form. Because of this you need at least one variety of round flowers in a design of mixed flowers to hold and focus the eye. There are lots of round flowers to choose from such as gerberas, chrysanthemums, carnations, open roses, or sunflowers.

Round leaves also have a special place in flower design, especially in a small arrangement where their plain form and texture give contrast and pull together an arrangement of mixed flowers and foliage. The larger the arrangement the less rounded the leaves need be.

■ Rhythm is created in this handtied through the repetition of round circular form. The mass of open *Tulipa* 'Angelique' are surrounded by a frill of asparagus fern and the whole is encapsulated by a three dimensional dome of steel grass. Tiny glass jewels have been placed in the centre of the tulips to heighten interest.

■ **Round forms.** rose chrysanthemum geranium ivy
(*Pelargonium*)

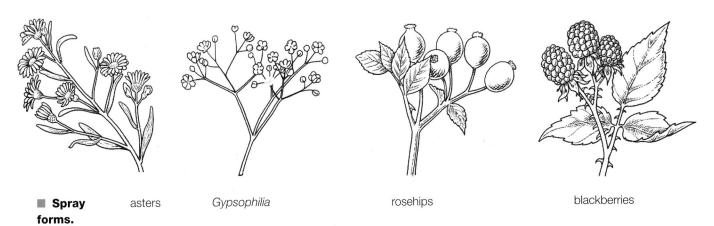

■ **Spray** asters *Gypsophilia* rosehips blackberries
forms.

Spray forms

Spray foliage, flowers and berries can give:

■ further interest to the design through their form
■ textural contrast, as in smooth *Hypericum* berries, hips or haws
■ a means of filling in the design inexpensively.

Solidago, Alchemilla mollis, Alstroemeria, cow parsley, *Hypericum*, rose hips, and privet berries are but a few examples.

■ The textures of smooth berries, coarse hairy wool, lichen encrusted bark, granular *Erica*, sinuous vine trails, and fluffy rough *Allium porrum* meet on a rusty metal grid.

Texture

Texture refers to how we imagine a flower or leaf will feel to the touch. Interest in an arrangement is intensified by the selection of different textures which contrast with each other.

Think of a teasel – how do you imagine it would feel to the touch? Prickly is the word we use to describe its texture.

Smooth texture

It is important to include at least one foliage or flower with a smooth texture in all arrangements of mixed flowers and foliage. The smooth texture holds together all the other elements and can be found in leaves such as ivy *(Hedera)*, Boston ivy (*Parthenocissus tricuspicata)*, round leaved *Eucalyptus*, *Aspidistra* and *Hosta*, in seedheads and berries and in many round composite flowers such as *Cosmos*, marguerites, and *Rudbeckia*. Fruit and vegetables, which can be easily incorporated into a design, may also give a smooth texture.

■ A contrast of two textures and two forms. Smooth *Hypericum* 'Excellent Flair' are massed against clipped palms.

Arrangements where texture is of extra importance

When arrangements are monochromatic (see page 36), or composed solely of dried materials, there is a special need for exciting textural contrasts.

Colour

Complete books have been written on colour. They are of immense value to those wanting to study this fascinating subject in depth. Here, however, is a brief summary of how to choose colour combinations and how colour can be used to interpret mood and to enhance the decor of your home.

Colour is perhaps the most emotive and important part of design as a whole and is a never ceasing wonder of exciting and dynamic permutations and combinations.

Using colour

The tips below will help you when choosing flowers of harmonizing colours to suit the occasion.

Link colours by using green

Green is the flower arrangers neutral colour. Whatever flowers you choose, such as red roses, yellow *Alstroemeria* and orange *Gerbera*, the combination will work if you add lots of plain green foliage.

Lime green adds vitality

Lime green flowers such as *Alchemilla mollis*, chrysanthemum 'Kermit' and bells of Ireland (*Molucella laevis*) will give zing and harmonize with all the other colours of the rainbow.

Add light to dark and dark to light

If your arrangement is predominantly of pastel colours introduce some dark foliage to give depth and heighten interest. Conversely, if the arrangement is of dark subdued colours introduce a touch of a lighter tint to give vitality or place the arrangement against a light background.

Link flowers to the seasons

Colours are linked to the seasons, both in the mind and in what is seasonally available. Traditionally we think of blue, yellow and pink in the spring, mixed colours in the summer, strong deep tones of yellow, orange, pink and terracotta for the autumn and red, green, white and gold during the winter months.

■ Right: Blue and yellow signal the onset of spring. On an Oasis ring yellow *Gerbera*, *Rosa* var., *Skimmia*, *Anemone*, *Camellia*, *Trachelium caeruleum*, *Solidaster*, *Thuja* sp. and *Fatshedera* (hybrid) *lizei* 'Variegata' are woven together to give a fresh and vital design.

■ In a design of dark colours, the addition of a tint gives life and vitality. *Ruscus hypophyllum*, *Cyperus papyrus* and dark red *Gerbera* are lifted by the addition of *Paeonia* 'Sarah Bernhardt' and lime green *Molucella laevis* (bells of Ireland).

Consider the location

Colour needs to be considered when arranging flowers in a large setting. Blues and violets recede and disappear when viewed from a distance. Conversely, warm colours such as reds, oranges and warm yellows advance and can be seen much more clearly. They can be used to great effect in a room that you want to appear smaller and more intimate.

Consider the lighting

Tungsten or electric lighting enhances reds, oranges and yellows but takes all the life out of blue flowers.

Fluorescent lighting has changed over the past few years and you can now purchase tubes that throw a light similar to daylight. Old fluorescent lighting gives a bluish cast which is great for blue flowers but not so good for reds, yellows and oranges.

Pastel colours show up best in candlelight. Receding colours such as blues and violets will disappear.

Link the colour with the container

As mentioned in Chapter 1 link the colour of the flowers you choose with the container. Copper and brass containers encourage the use of red, bronze and peach plant material. Aluminium and cream containers work well with white, cream and pink flowers. Blue flowers seem to work whatever the colour of the container.

Colours for special occasions

For Valentine's Day we think of red, for Christmas red, gold and green, and for Hallowe'en orange and black. Silver would be selected for a 25th wedding anniversary and pinks for the christening party of a baby girl. Today we often think in terms of white or cream for a traditional wedding.

Warm and cool colours

Reds, oranges, and gold yellows are warm colours and live happily together. Blues, purples and sharp yellows are cool colours and are harmonious in the same design.

■ Pink roses, cream 'Valarian' roses and *Tulipa* var. blend with grey *Eucalyptus* and *Hedera helix* berries in a grey metal container topped by a cream candle.

Colour combinations

The colour wheel is an fascinating part of the flower arrangers' world. The colour wheel uses three principal (primary) colours – red, blue and yellow (which are the only three colours which can not be obtained by mixing two or more colours together). These primary colours are mixed together to provide further colours. A straight mix of red and blue provides purple, blue and yellow produce green, and yellow and red make orange. Purple, green and orange are termed secondary colours.

Tints

Tints are acquired by adding white to the primary and secondary colours. For example a tint of red is pink, a tint of yellow is lemon. Another word for a tint is a pastel.

Shades

Shades are acquired by adding black to the colour. A shade of red is maroon. A shade of blue is navy.

Colour Schemes

Monochromatic colour scheme

A monochromatic colour scheme can use tints, shades and the full intensity of a single colour. Interest in the arrangement can be heightened by the use of strong textural contrasts.

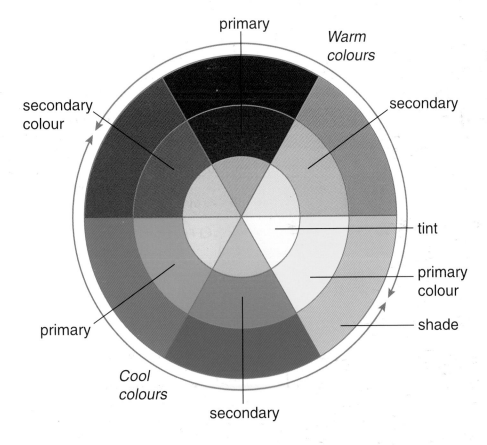

■ Colour wheel.

■ The warm colours of yellow, orange and red displayed by a group of vibrant poppies. The sprigs of *Spirea* flowers and creamy white poppies add vitality and link through the central boss of their yellow stamens. Chicken wire has been carefully wrapped around the inside of each of the glass tumblers to give contrast and interest.

Adjacent colour scheme

An adjacent colour scheme uses up to one-third of a colour wheel, the colours all being found next to each other. It is, however, understood in flower arranging that green may also be included. One example would be green-yellow, yellow, yellow-orange and orange, plus green.

Complementary colour scheme

If colours on opposite sides of the wheel are used together such as red and green or yellow and purple then a more dynamic colour scheme is achieved. Any two complementary colours used together intensify and so enhance each other brilliantly. Put blue flowers against an orange background and observe the clarity with which you enjoy the flowers. Avoid using equal amounts of two colours. Let one colour dominate so that the two colours do not vie and pull the eye in different directions. Conversely, do not use just one flower of a particular colour. A single yellow flower in a design of other colours will stick out like a sore thumb.

Polychromatic colour scheme

This is the use of many colours together. A polychromatic colour scheme is always cheerful and vibrant. The use of plain green foliage brings all the colours together harmoniously.

Principles of design

Space

Solid is the opposite of space; without space there is no form. The Japanese art of Ikebana makes good use of space and it is to this ancient art that many westerners turn for inspiration. Space can be incorporated into a flower arrangement in the following ways.

■ **Within the arrangement** Classic design incorporates space between the plant material using a greater amount of space at the limits of the design rather than at the stronger focal area, which is generally positioned just below the centre of the arrangement. The use of space allows different planes and angles to be incorporated and overall interest in the design is thus increased.

■ Two *Hippeastrum* sp. rise from a base of *Gypsophila* 'Million Stars' and *Galax urceolata* leaves, both contained within a simple framework of *Xanthorrhea australis* (steel grass) loops, capturing space within the design.

In a contemporary design of limited material, space can be used to balance form, colour and texture. Space can have as much eye-pull as a solid form, usually when enclosed by manipulation of leaves or loops of cane, raffia or plant material.

In massed contemporary deisgns there is little space within the design itself. However, space can be incorporated by placing plant material at varying levels, using bridge material such as driftwood or flexible grasses or simply by using volumetric flower forms with space within.

- **Underneath the container** In both classic and contemporary designs, space underneath the container can be used to give a sense of lightness and grace.

- **In the setting** It is vital to position you arrangement so that it is surrounded by space; here space is allied to proportion and scale. Perhaps the easiest way to illustrate this point is to imagine a niche. The arrangement should fill approximately two thirds of the space and no more. Conversely the arrangement should not be so small in proportion to its surroundings that it becomes insignificant.

Balance

A flower arrangement should have physical balance and visual balance.

Physical balance

Physical balance means that the arrangement must not topple over. To prevent this happening the container or vase must be large enough for the amount of flowers that you are using and your mechanics must be sound and secure. Your Oasis should be fully charged with water but not over soaked. If it is it will crumble as you insert your final stems. You also need to ensure that the flowers are evenly distributed in the arrangement so the weight is not one-sided.

Visual balance

If your arrangement is unlikely to fall over but looks as if it might, the visual balance needs adjusting. The arrangement will only be pleasing to the eye if there is stability in the arrangement and doesn't make you feel anxious.

■ A variegated *Phormium tenax* leaf is curled around a single rose in a tube and placed within a glass container. Space abounds within the container but is closely linked to the guidelines of good proportion.

Types of balance

Symmetrical balance

True symmetrical balance is achieved when one side of the arrangement is identical to the other side – one side is the mirror image of the other. Flower arranging is, however, less contrived and the term symmetrical balance is used when one side approximates the other. The visual weight is approximately the same but the flowers and foliage used on each side are not identical.

Symmetrical arrangements are used in a setting where the areas exposed on each side are similar – such as on the centre of a table or the centre of a mantelpiece.

Asymmetrical balance

Asymmetrical balance is harder to understand and harder to achieve. The visual weight of the plant material is different each side of the central axis. Although the elements are different, balance is achieved by each side having equal eye attraction. The arrangement on page 40 has asymmetric balance.

Tips for achieving good balance

- Rounded forms usually appear heavier than linear forms.
- Rounded fruits and vegetables give both visual and actual weight so be careful when placing them in a front-facing arrangement.
- Visual weight increases the further the materials are from the central axis, the stronger they are in colour, the warmer they are in hue and the larger the form.
- Colours that advance such as yellows and oranges have more visual strength than colours which recede.
- Shiny textures have more draw than dull textures.

■ The two placements of clipped palms, *Aspidistra* and lilies provides an example of asymmetric balance.

Scale

Scale is the relationship between each element of the design and each individual piece of plant material.

- It is important to consider the size of each flower and stem of foliage in relation to each other. A hydrangea would not rest comfortably with a daisy. Lily of the valley would feel outsized by a Kentia palm.
- The size of the container holding your plant material should be in scale in size and texture.
- Think of the setting in which your arrangement will be displayed. A large hall has need of a large

An eggcup holds snippets of *Muscari*, polyanthus, *Lamium* sp., *Ribes* flowers, *Myosotis* (forget-me-not), *Cupressus macrocarpa* 'Gold Crest' and cow parsley. The plant material is in scale with each other and also with the size of the container.

arrangement with bold plant material. The rooms of a small flat would be in scale with an arrangement of smaller flowers and foliage.

Proportion

Proportion is the word that is used to describe one part of your arrangement to the other parts and to the arrangement as a whole.

The foundations for good proportions were laid down by the Ancient Greeks. Their discoveries, sometimes called the *golden section* or the *golden mean*, have withstood the test of time and give pleasing results today as in yesteryear. The formula is applied to the proportions of the human body: AC is to AB as CB is to AC. This theory also applies to areas and volumes.

AC is to AB as CB is to AC

- The *golden section* or *golden mean*.

Transferring the *golden mean* into flower arranging guidelines can be broadly summed up by considering either volume (when there is a mass of plant material) or height (when relatively few stems are involved). This is not as difficult as it sounds.

Volume

If you have a mass of plant material, think in terms of volume – that is the relationship in volume between the plant material and the container. Either the flowers or the container should dominate and the relationship between the two parts should be one and

a half to one. There should never be equal eye pull demanded by both parts of the overall design, however harmonious it might be in terms of colour, form and texture.

Height

If you have only relatively few stems think in terms of height:

- If your container is low your tallest stem should be about one and a half times the width of the container.
- If your container is tall your height should be about one and a half times the height of the container.

Positioning of flowers

You should also consider if your flowers are in proportion to their setting. Very simply this means that for a large reception you would not use a thimble containing wild flowers. This is closely linked with scale.

Rhythm

Rhythm is perhaps the hardest of the principles to explain. Perhaps it is best understood by using the word 'movement'. In an arrangement with good rhythm the eye is moved along through the arrangement by the following means.

■ The curling movement of the silver ting ting gives rhythm to this design of *Hebe* 'Mrs Winder', *Pittosporum* 'Tom Thumb' and 'Irene Patterson' and *Dianthus* 'Arevalo'.

■ Left: The plant material is approximately one and a half times the volume of the container, and gives pleasing proportions. The colour and the material of the container are visually heavy and so the proportions could be slightly exaggerated. The height of the plant material is also approximately one and a half times the height of the container.

■ Rhythm is created from the upward surge of stems which flow into a mass of undulating exotic leaf fronds of *Philodendron* 'Xanadu' and the twisting stems of the longlasting *Ornithogalum arabicum* (Arabian chincherinchees).

■ At an exhibition in Holland three containers filled with apples and branches of rose hips give rhythm through repetition.

Repetition

Repetition of colours, forms, textures and space takes the eye through the design. The eye instinctively looks for association and is led through the design. Repeating the form of a leaf by overlapping leaves of the same variety creates movement which heightens interest.

Radiating lines

Radiation is one of the most pleasing means of creating good rhythm. Lines that flow uninterrupted from a central point give a feeling of movement. This feeling is dispelled if any of the lines cross and the rhythm is interrupted.

Transition

The graduation of size, form and colour leads the eye gently into and out of the arrangement.

■ Overleaf: Contrast of form. Round focal *Rosa* 'Grand Prix' contrast strongly with the linear chilli peppers despite the colour being the same.

Contrast

Contrast is the difference shown when objects are placed next to each other. When using different forms and textures the contrast can be obvious but there is also subtle contrast when a mass of flowers of the same variety are placed in a vase. The contrast is then based on the different length of the stems and the flowers in their various states of development.

Contrast of form

When using more than one type of plant material avoid arranging similar materials that do not have sufficient contrast. Always use at least one flower with a round form.

Contrast of colour

Complimentary colours make the strongest contrast. If the colours have gentle contrast strong contrasts of form and texture are often needed.

Contrast of texture

Strong textural contrasts are often needed in monochromatic designs.

Dominance

If a flower design contains two or more equal attractions they will pull the design apart. Without dominance there is lack of unity and harmony. Dominance provides a sense of order. Dominance is often linked to proportion.

There should always be:

- Dominant texture. A smooth shiny texture is more compelling than a rough texture. Always allow one texture to dominate.
- Dominant movement. Dominant movement or line directions can perhaps be most clearly seen by looking at the photographs of the layered arrangement on page 106–7 and the parallel arrangement on page 87. If the movement was equally upright and along in either of these cases the result would be discord.
- Dominant form. Round is the most dominant form by virtue of eye attraction and weight. When adding spray and linear forms to a design there should be a sufficient number of other forms to be in good proportion visually.
- Dominant colour. Pale colours are more dominant than darker colours. Therefore if you use a combination of light and dark ensure that these are also in good proportion.

■ The *Heuchera* leaves and single rose dominate the tall spires of the *Heuchera* flower. The strong form, depth of colour and limited space creates greater impact over height and space.

5

Classic design

The classic style has been enjoyed since the 1930s. It brings the English garden indoors, in the spirit of a time when an abundance of flowers and foliage could be picked from the garden. Despite smaller gardens and the pressure of time today, the classic English style can still be enjoyed with a mixture of garden plant material and florists' flowers and foliage.

■ Fragrant garden roses, mint and sweet-smelling geranium leaves arranged in a low round basket.

Characteristics

- The different designs are all loosely based on a geometric form.
- In each design every stem radiates or appears to radiate from a central point.
- The designs are usually dependent on garden plant material using buds, half-open and full-blown flowers with curving branches of foliage.
- The plant material is usually scattered through the design but the colours, forms and textures are woven to lead the eye gently through. This adds to the rhythmic quality of the design.
- There is a more dominant area at the base of the tallest stem, approximately two thirds of the way down the design. This can be achieved with larger forms, stronger colour or the use of a different texture.
- There are no strong surprises or contrasts. Variation is soft and gradual.
- There is a certain amount of space between each element of plant material to show each and every form to advantage.
- The container is sometimes hidden or of classic design.

General guidelines

The following guidelines will help you create successful classic designs. They are not rules but tips that work and will build up your confidence.

- Foliage is generally used to create the outline. The outline is reinforced by other plant material.
- All stems should appear to radiate from one small area in the centre of the foam – this has been referred to as 'X' in the illustrations on the following pages. The stems do not actually originate from this point (if they did you would have an awful lot of stems criss-crossing over each other in a small piece of foam). They simply give the impression of radiating from point 'X'.
- For good visual balance bolder forms should be lower in the design but not so low that they appear to be falling out. Bold forms (such as *Gerbera*) need to have a leaf positioned underneath so that neutral green is at the perimeter.
- A round flower form is essential in each and every design to hold together all the other elements in the design.
- All arrangements should include some plant material with a smooth texture.
- Recessing some of the plant material gives depth and interest. Recessing means placing some plant material closer to the foam to give a strong 3D effect.
- Only insert the minimum length of stem to keep it securely in position.
- As a large amount of plant material is used ensure you have a reserve of water in your container at all times.

Table arrangements

Table arrangements should be either tall enough to see under or low enough to see over. In Victorian times the taller arrangements were much in evidence, overflowing with ferns, trails of ivy and a profusion of flowers and fruit. Today the size of our homes and perhaps the increased pressures in our lives call for a smaller, lower arrangement that can be created easily yet is effective and is a pleasure to observe. For the grand occasion, with the larger table, a two tier arrangement has tremendous impact and takes up no more space on the table.

A table arrangement should be in good proportion to the size of the table. As a very rough guide no more than one fifth of the table should be covered. If the table is rectangular and for more than eight people, two smaller arrangements at either end of the table, are more practical and can be enjoyed by all.

Plant material used for table arrangements should be in perfect condition for the very good reason that it will be subjected to close scrutiny. Your arrangement should be part of the overall effect created by the table setting. Choose flowers which will repeat a colour in your china or pottery and which will harmonise with the table linen. If the occasion is grand choose more sophisticated flowers such as the orchid and the lily rather than the carnation. If the setting is informal, perhaps in the kitchen, choose flowers such as daisy chrysanthemums and introduce fruits and vegetables.

Round table arrangement

As a flower arranger you will be asked to create a round table arrangement more frequently than any other style. According to the flowers and foliage used this arrangement can be enjoyed from any angle.

You will need:

- A low waterproof dish. For your first attempts this should be about 12 cm (5 in) in diameter. If your container is porous line it with thick polythene such as a section of bin liner. This will create an arrangement for a table for six to eight people.
- A piece of floral foam. A third of a block will be a good approximate size.
- Florists' tape to keep the foam securely in place.
- Outline foliage. This could be privet, *Ribes* (flowering currant) or tree ivy from the garden or hard *Ruscus*, *Eucalyptus cinerea* or *Gaultheria shallon* (salal) from the florist.
- Approximately 7–9 round concealer leaves such as ivy, geranium, *Heuchera* from the garden or *Galax* from the florist.
- Around 7 outline flowers such as roses in bud, spray carnations, neat *Solidaster* sprays.
- Roughly 5–7 round focal flowers such as mini *Gerbera*, open roses, chrysanthemums.
- Filler flowers and foliage, including some spray material, such as cow parsley, rose hips, berries, *Hypericum*, variegated *Pittosporum*, *Viburnum tinus*, *Alstroemeria*, *Gypsophila*, or spray chrysanthemums.

Creating the design

1 Soak the foam for about 60 seconds (see page 17). Place the foam in the dish and secure well using either a frog and fix or florists' tape (or both for larger arrangements). The foam must rise well above the rim of the container.

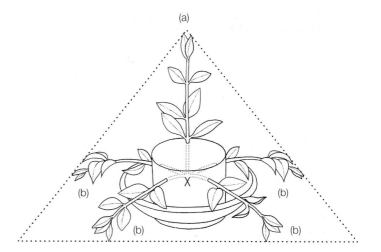

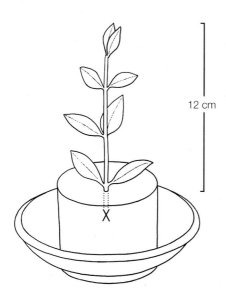

2 Place a stem of foliage in position (*a*). It should be central in the foam. For your first attempt use foliage which rises approximately 12 cm (4.5 in) from the foam.

3 Place stems in position (*b*). These will be the same length as stem (*a*). It is suggested that when starting out you use the same plant foliage for the entire outline at this stage. These stems should be inserted about halfway up the foam and angled slightly downwards over the rim of the container. Angle them so that if they appear to originate from point X. This is very important. Sometimes it is difficult to know how many stems to use. A rough guideline is to use sufficient stems so that the first leaves on the stem emerging from the foam almost touch the ones next door.

4 Place an odd number of stems (*c*) with the stem length as (*a*) and (*b*) out of the top of the foam. Avoid placing these directly above the material which you have already inserted. Place these stems in between those already in position.

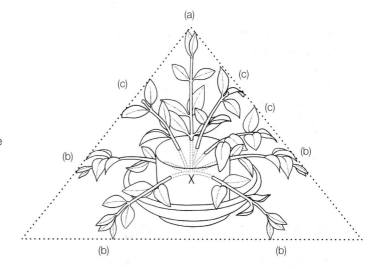

5 At this stage it is important that these stems stay within the boundaries of the dotted line triangle shown below. Check that all stems appear to come from the same point of origin (X) within the foam.

6 At this stage add your round concealer leaves. Avoid a frilly effect by inserting stems so that the leaves lie at different angles. Vary the stem lengths so that the overall form is reinforced throughout. At this point you will be able to see a small amount of foam but there should be a good strong skeleton of foliage.

7 Now add line flowers almost to the limits of the design and throughout. Your first placement should reinforce the central stem and be straight upright. If it is angled away from this central vertical position it will be difficult to achieve a well-balanced design. Try at this point to not go beyond the outline created by your foliage. All stems should appear to radiate from point X (see earlier illustrations). At this point pick up your arrangement and look at it at eye level. Check that some stems are being angled downwards over the rim of the container.

8 Place the round focal flowers at intervals throughout your arrangement. The round flowers will vary in size, to some extent. Consequently, position the smaller flowers higher in the design and the larger flowers more centrally. Again avoid creating a frill of flowers – show them off at different angles at different heights. Do not cut the stems too short. Lift your arrangement to eye level to check that plant material flows over the rim of the container and that the flowers are not just in the top two thirds of the arrangement.

9 Add filler material to complete. If this material is light and airy it might well extend beyond the outline. Keep within the framework established by the line material.

10 Ensure that your container always has a reservoir of water.

■ Round table arrangement. *Arachniodes adantiformis* (leather leaf) gives the outline, *Parthenocissus tricuspidata* the concealer leaves, *Solidago* the line flowers, *Rosa* sp. the focal flowers and *Asparagus umbellatus* (Ming fern) the filler material.

■ In this round table arrangement *Eucalyptus cinerea* forms the outline, *Heuchera micrantha* leaves help conceal the foam, neat *Syringa* sprays give the linear flowers, *Rosa* the focal interest and *Nigella damascena* (love-in-a-mist), *Hordeum vulgare* (barley), *Eustoma grandiflorum* (lisianthus) and *Anthriscus sylvestris* (cow parsley) seedheads provide filler material.

Variations

Create an individual container for your all-round arrangement by:

■ Wrapping wide double-sided tape around a plastic bowl and sticking on lengths of snake grass.
■ Taking a basket and removing the handle. Use a

couple of trails of well-conditioned ivy to wrap round the rim, securing with short lengths of wire to the basket.
■ Filling a basket or attractive container with a mass of fruiting tree ivy to fully cover the foam. Simply add an array of flowers in colours of your choice.
■ Adding a candle centrally.

Oval table arrangement

This arrangement is suitable for an oval or rectangular table. It can also be easily adapted for a top table or mantelpiece (see Variations).

You will need:

- One third of a brick of foam.
- A shallow container. The foam must rise above the rim of the container and fill no more than half to two thirds of the container.
- Outline foliage such as small-leaved ivy sprays, *Hebe*, beech from the garden or *Ruscus*, *Gaultheria shallon* (salal), or *Eucalyptus* from the florist.
- Outline flowers such as spray carnations.
- Round concealing leaves to give a smooth texture such as *Tolmeia*, round ivy leaves, *Fatshedera* or *Galax*.
- Focal flowers.
- Filler foliage or flowers, including spray material.

Creating the design

1 Place the foam in the dish and secure well. The foam should have been soaked as described on page 17. Place a stem of outline foliage centrally, in position (*a*) as shown below. For your first attempt use foliage that rises about 12 cm (4.5 in) above the level of the foam. Place two stems of the same line material in both long ends of the foam, position (*b*), a third longer than stem (*a*), i.e. approximately 16 cm long. You have now formed the triangle ABC. BC is about 42 cm long (2 × 16 cm plus 10 cm for the width of the foam). Therefore, your completed arrangement will be about 42 cm long.

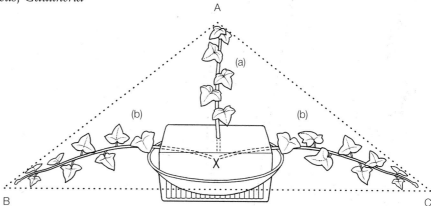

2 Place two short pieces of outline foliage in position (c). Repeat on the other side. These stems should be approximately half the length of (b), i.e. 8 cm from the foam. At this point check that every stem appears to have the same point of origin X. There should be approximately the same spacing between all the lower placements.

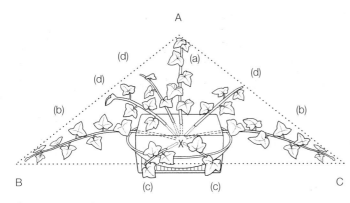

3 Place an odd number of stems (d) (see above) in the top and sides of the foam. They should be about the same length as (c) – approximately 8 cm long. At this point do not have any material protruding outside the dotted line triangle. Once again check that all stems appear to come from the same point of origin X. Place stems (d) above the spaces between the lower placements and not directly in a line above them.

4 Add round concealer leaves to cover some of the foam and dish rim. Avoid a frilly effect by inserting stems at different angles. Reinforce all the outline form and not just the central area. You should now have a good strong outline. The foam will show but will not be too evident.

5 Add line flowers almost to the limit of the design and throughout the design. Place the first flower so that it reinforces the first vertical placement of the foliage. Put the stems at regular intervals to avoid wide open spaces. Pay particular attention to the area between placements (b) and (c) (refer to illustration top left). Add extra outline material if needed to give a smoother flow.

6 Place the round focal flowers at intervals through the arrangement. Avoid a tendency to have an all-round arrangement with two arms attached as shown in the line drawing below. The smallest focal flowers should be closer to the edges, the largest in the centre and the others in between.

Incorrect X

Correct ✓

7 Add filler material to complete, including spray flowers or berries. If unsure keep within the framework established by the line material.

8 Ensure that your arrangement always has water in the bottom of your container.

■ An oval arrangement in a low dish. The outline has been created with *Ribes sanguineum* (flowering currant foliage). *Parthenocissus tricuspidata* are the round leaves, *Rosa* sp. (roses) the focal flowers. *Hebe*, *Rubus fruticosus* (blackberries), *Papaver orientalis* (poppy) seedheads, *Achillea millefolium*, *Verbena* and *Buddleja* fill the arrangement.

■ An oval design in a bark container. The autumnal mood is reinforced by the addition of mini terracotta pots filled with beans and pulses.

■ Left: This oval design has a candle inserted in the centre of the arrangement which consists of *Eucalyptus cinerea*, *Solidago*, *Rosa* sp., *Chrysanthemum* 'Kermit' and *Ribes* with autumnal tints. Terracotta pots filled with beans and pulses complete the design.

Variations

■ For a top table or mantelpiece arrangement the outline is exactly the same but two long 'arms' will be longer and curve down over the rim of the table or mantelpiece. The triangular form ABC has a curved base. Ensure that you respect this line and that your long stems do not become awkward arms.

■ Fruits and vegetables add interest to table arrangements and are so simple to incorporate. Take wooden cocktail or kebab sticks. Impale into the fruit with two or three lengths according to the weight and then add to the arrangement.

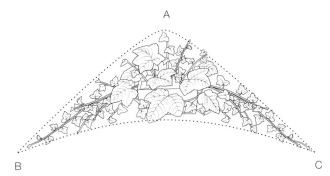

■ This mantelpiece arrangement is a variation of the oval design. This design is quick and simple to complete and always looks effective. The outline material for this arrangement is *Taxus baccata* (yew) complemented by *Camellia* foliage, *Viburnum tinus*, *Betula* twigs, *Pinus* (pine) cones, limes, *Dianthus* and *Hypericum*.

Crescents

The downward crescent

The downward crescent is light and graceful. It gives a sophisticated arrangement using the minimal amount of plant material. As it is in a raised container it can be placed where space is at a premium. You can use a glass bottle, a candlestick or a tall, relatively slim container. A bottle can be filled with water to give extra stability.

Try to find a container that is between 25 cm (10 in) and 35 cm (14 in) high. An arrangement on a 25 cm (10 in) tall container will use smaller-sized material than one 35 cm (14 in) high. Trails of neat ivy, pinks, florists' roses and *Alchemilla mollis* would be in scale with the smaller container but larger ivies and generous garden roses would be more appropriate for a larger container.

A candlecup should be attached to your container securely with florists' fix and florists' tape.

You will need:

- A piece of foam. The foam should rise at least 2.5 cm above the rim of the container.
- A tall container, candlestick or bottle.
- Candlecup or a dish that will fit securely in the container's opening.
- A candle (optional), cocktail sticks and tape.
- Curved line material (this design will not work with straight line material) such as honeysuckle, lengths of ivy, *Eucalyptus* or broom.
- Flexible line flowers or flowers that can be pruned to make a curve. These may not be needed if blossom or flowering line foliage is used for the outline.
- Round concealer leaves such as round ivy leaves, Boston ivy, geranium (*Pelargonium*) or *Galax*.
- Round, focal flowers such as open roses, marigolds, mini *Gerbera*.
- Filler material such as *Alstroemeria*, *Viburnum tinus*, *Alchemilla mollis*, *Solidaster* (hybrid).

Creating the design

1 Place the foam in the candlecup or dish and secure well.
2 If using a candle, prepare as on page 22 and insert in the centre of the foam.
3 Insert a length of line material (a) centrally. If using a candle it should be no more than half the length of the candle. Stem (a) is short. On a 25 cm (10 in) tall container the tallest stem would be about 10 cm (4 in) and no more. This is a crescent and the finished design should have the form of a crescent moon.

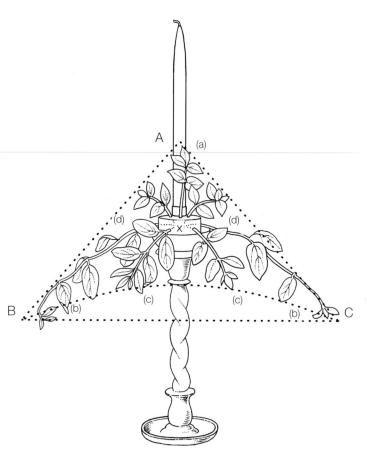

4 Insert curved outline material (*b*) into the sides of the foam so that it flows downwards. The stems should be inserted in the top half of the foam and angled downwards. You have now formed the shape ABC. Each stem should be about twice the length of (*a*). If straightened they will also be approximately the same length as the container's height. The curve in the stem and the angle at which they are placed will mean they fall well short of the base.

5 Add shorter stems (*c*) also angled downwards. Their stem ends should appear to have the same imaginary origin X. Repeat on the far side. These should be about one third the length of placements (*b*). They should just reach over the rim of the container and a little beyond.

6 Insert short stems (*d*) in the top of the foam, all apparently arising from the same point in the foam X. Do not go outside the dotted line triangle.

7 Use plain round concealer leaves to hide the mechanics and to provide a restful contrast to the other material. A relatively large leaf placed low and centrally is well placed to complement a focal flower(s).

8 Take line flowers through the design, stopping short of the boundaries.

9 Insert focal flowers low in the arrangement and slightly recessed. The larger flowers should be placed in the central area graduating outwards to the smallest flowers. If the arrangement is to be placed against a wall use your best blooms at the front.

10 Add filler material to complete the design. As in the oval table arrangement ensure that the two long stems are not isolated. Graduate the material so that the design has unity. Do not worry if you feel that only a little is needed – you are probably right.

Variations

Creating a round raised arrangement that can be viewed all round, rather than a crescent, is very simple. Place the foam and candle in the raised container as shown previously in the illustration. Insert flowing plant material, of approximately the same length, all round the foam.

If you have a tall container you may wish to place the base inside a ring which you will cover with plant material to give a two-tier arrangement.

■ A simple design in a glass candlestick. *Hedera helix* provides the outline. *Rosa* foliage complements the focal roses, *Dianthus* 'Doris' and *Deutzia*.

Upward crescent

The upward crescent is a stylised but effective design that uses only a small amount of plant material. Unlike the classic downward crescent, which has sides of approximately the same length, the upward crescent looks better when one side is longer than the other. It is usual to follow a generous curve of the new moon.

This design cannot be created without curved line material so if you cannot find any, create another style of arrangement. However, some plant material can be encouraged to curve. Broom can be soaked for a couple of hours and then tied in the required shape. When dried it will be permanently curved but make sure you do not overdo it or else you will find you have created a circle. Blossom is ideal as it takes colour and flowers to the limits of the design without the addition of extra stems which can muddle the outline. Flowering japonica or quince (*Chaenomeles*) often has lovely curves. Flexible plant material such as willow or dogwood can be encouraged to bend using warm hands.

The plant material needs to be kept firmly in place and although you can use foam, a pinholder is recommended. If the stems are in foam they can swing round. A pinholder can easily be covered either with plant material, moss or small pebbles. Covering foam can lead to a fussy effect that is bottom heavy and this destroys the clarity of the overall form.

You will need:

- A pinholder with a 6.25 cm (2.5 in) diameter (a larger or smaller pinholder will also work).
- Fix.
- A low, shallow container large enough to take the pinholder and which allows the pins to be covered by water.
- Some flat pebbles or moss to hide the pinholder (optional).
- Curved line material such as broom, rosemary, blossom, pussy willow, forsythia.
- Line flowers with curved stems (if you are using blossom this may not be necessary).
- Round leaves.
- Round, focal flowers.
- Spray material.

Creating the design

1   Place a stem of curved plant material in the pinholder (*a*). This should be approximately twice the length of the shallow container.

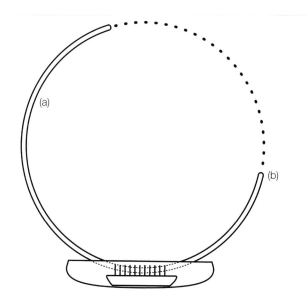

2 The second stem of curved material (*b*) should be about two thirds the length of (*a*) and should be placed so that the imaginary dotted line shown in the diagram would approximately complete the circle.

3 If you have used fine stems to create the outline reinforce with shorter stems.

4 Use a few round leaves to partially conceal the pinholder. Always bear in mind the clean-cut sickle effect you are creating.

5 Line flowers can reinforce the shape but do not try to do the impossible with stems that are too rigid such as *Iris* or with buds that will open later to spoil your outline. Keep your colour scheme reasonably simple. If, for example, yellow is used for your focal flowers make sure that the colour is extended through your design, perhaps using yellow spray carnations as line material.

6 Create the tip of the focal area. This should be in the area at the base of the tallest stem. If stem (*a*) does not come over as far as the centre of the pinholder your focal area may be slightly off-centre. Only use one or two round flowers at this point. If possible place a few smaller flowers and their buds further into the curve to link the outer parts of the design with the centre so that the design is a harmonious whole.

7 If necessary, complete the shape with spray material. This is not always required.

8 Look at your design and remove any pieces of plant material which are superfluous. Check that you do not have an accumulation of leaves at the base which would spoil the smooth line of the curve. Space and a clear-cut outline are very important as less really is more in this design. Cover any mechanics which still show with moss or flat pebbles rather than plant material.

Triangles

The symmetrical triangle

The classic symmetrical triangle is less frequently seen than in the past. However, it is still as popular as a pedestal arrangement, for large open areas such as churches and hotel receptions as it is the only really effective way of displaying an abundance of plant material to be seen and enjoyed by a large audience from three sides.

Key points for arranging the symmetric triangle

- The container and/or pedestal must be integrated into the overall design. This is achieved by angling plant material downwards over the rim and down the top of the container or pedestal.
- In order to gain the greatest interest in your design allow your flowers to face all directions. Look at a plant and observe how the flowers and leaves do this. All angles of flowers are interesting and a combination of angles gives variety.
- Try not to create a flat arrangement. Depth or a strong three-dimensional form will create interest and hold the eye. Depth can be created in different ways:
  - The back of your arrangement should be built up with foliage and flowers and not left bare even though it may be standing close to a wall. It does not have to hold the best blooms but do include some colour as its presence will always be felt.
  - Recess some of your flowers and foliage. Shorter stems, usually of bolder material, are positioned closer to the foam. Recessing also takes emphasis away from a 'stemmy' effect which is often created by using flowers such as carnations which have a small proportion of flower head to stem.

You will need:

- A raised container. The flowers need to be raised so that a graceful downward relaxed effect can be achieved. A flat bowl makes the design static.
- Foam to fit your container. This could be wedged into the opening. You could alternatively place a low dish in the opening in which to place your foam. Ensure there is room for a reservoir of water. This could be secured with a frog and fix and/or a length of florists' tape.
- Line material. The plant material should not be too finely linear as you need to create a strong structure without too many stems as these would fill the foam too quickly and give an over fussy appearance.
- Line flowers.
- Focal flowers.
- Round concealer leaves, for example, *Fatshedera*, *Tellima*, geranium (*Pelargonium*) or ivy leaves. For larger symmetrical triangles less rounded, longer leaves will work well and take smooth texture higher through the design.
- Filler spray material such as *Hypericum* berries or *Alstroemeria*.

Creating the design

1 Place a piece of line material (*a*) about one and a half times the height of the container in the top of the foam centrally and two thirds of the way back. This stem should not lean forward.
2 Place stems (*b*) half to two thirds the length of (*a*) sideways out of the foam, forwards and slightly, angled downwards. This flow of plant material below the rim of the container prevents the arrangement looking as if it is unhappily perched on a stand. A gentle curve to the plant material will make this design look more natural and avoid the design appearing to have two ungainly arms.
3 Add two stems (*c*), approximately half the length of stem (*a*), out of the top of the foam. They should not protrude outside the boundary of the triangle. If they do go beyond this boundary they must be reduced even if they are only half the length of (*a*).

4   At this point check that all stems seem to originate from the imaginary point X deep in the foam.

5   Add two short stems (*d*) about half the length of (*b*), at the front and back of the design, angled downwards and outwards.

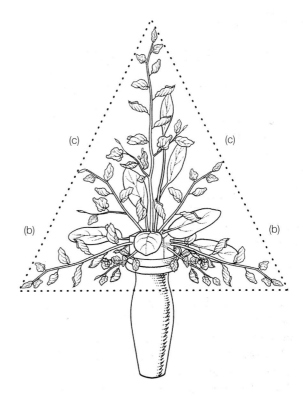

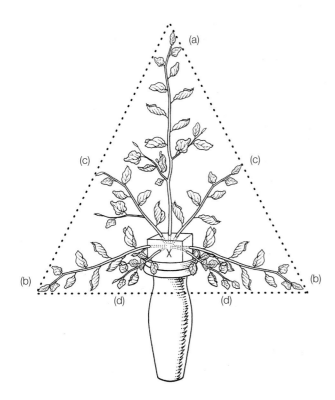

6   Give depth to the design by adding a stem of foliage and/or flowers behind the central stem. This will be shorter than the main stem and angled slightly backwards.

7   Use smooth-textured concealer leaves to cover some of the foam and container rim. Use some leaves on longer stems so that they are not all at the base of the design but taken through the central two thirds of the triangle.

8   Reinforce the shape with line flowers but do not go beyond the boundaries of the triangle. Take additional line flowers through the design, front and back.

9   Create the focal area with round flowers such as open roses or mini gerbera – which are much easier to use than their big brother the *Gerbera* – in the central two thirds of the arrangement. Do not place your focal flowers too neatly. Turn them to show off all the angles of the flowers.

10 Complete the design with filler flowers and filler foliage.

11 To create a narrower triangle angle stems (*b*) more sharply and reduce the length of stem (*c*) to fit the triangle.

■ A symmetrical triangle created with an outline of *Eucalyptus* 'Baby Blue' with *Fatsia japonica* concealer leaves. The open lilies (*Lilium* 'Pompeii') give focal interest. If the lilies were closed the deisgn would lack impact and interest. Other materials are *Fatsia* berries, lisianthus and *Euonymus* foliage.

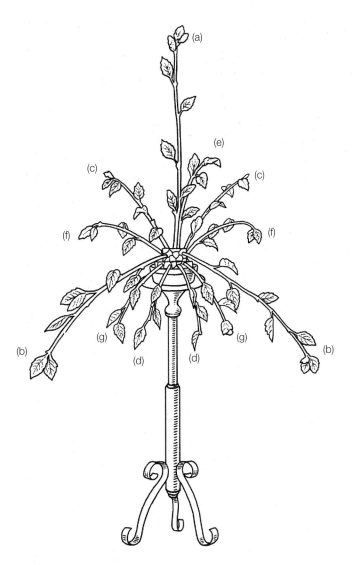

Variation: The pedestal arrangement

The typical church pedestal used to be a wrought iron stand which always seemed rather flimsy for the amount of plant material it supported. Today, it is possible to purchase inexpensive plywood pedestals which are strong and robust and give good balance for the wealth of plant material it will bear.

You will need:

- A green plastic bulb bowl or a small, round washing-up bowl approximately 20 cm (8 in) wide and 10 cm (4 in) deep is ideal for a moderate sized pedestal.
- Two blocks of foam. The full block can be placed upright on a frog at the back of the bowl. The second block can be positioned sideways in front of the first block. Any excess can be removed and used to wedge the foam firmly in position. The foam needs to rise well above the rim of the container. You will however need to leave space for the spout of a watering can to add water. Since you will be using a copious amount of plant material, water will need to be added regularly.
- A length of 2.5 cm (1 in) mesh chicken wire to reinforce your mechanics. This is particularly needed if you are planning to use woody stems. Cut the amount needed to make a cap over your foam. This can be kept firmly in place with reel wire, florists' tape or large rubber bands. If you are using rubber bands interloop them under the bowl and bring them up over the foam and netting to keep the netting in place. Refer to the line drawing on page 18.
- You will need bold plant material in scale with the stand and situation. *Rhododendron*, beech, dogwood (*Cornus*), flowering currant, *Camellia* and Kentia palms are excellent as line material and create a full outline simply and inexpensively. Outline flowers could be *Euphorbia fulgens*, carnations or *Delphinium*. Smooth-textured leaves could be *Aspidistra*, *Hosta*, croton and *Dracaena*. Bloom chrysanthemums, *Gerbera*, hydrangeas could be your focal flowers and *Hypericum*, *Alstroemeria*, *Solidaster* or *Solidago* filler material.
- Create the design as for the symmetrical triangle but ensure that your plant material drapes copiously downwards all the way round to give depth and movement.

The asymmetric triangle

The asymmetric triangle is one of the most pleasing of classic designs. It is usually positioned on one side of a chest, mantelpiece, altar or table rather than centrally. It is often used to balance an ornament or lamp.

In symmetric design the two sides positioned on the left and right of the central axis are more or less the same. In asymmetric design the left and right sides of the central axis are different. They differ:

- in the size of the plant material used;
- in the form of the plant material used;
- in the use of space.

The area 'Y' contains:

- fewer stems;
- larger plant material;
- uses less space.

than area 'Z'.

You will need:

- A low dish or bowl, or one that is slightly raised.
- Foam – one third of a block is ample. Chamfer the corners.
- A four-pronged disc and fix.
- Line material. The tallest stem, which will establish the height, should have a gentle curve, such as broom, *Escallonia*, ivy, holly or *Eucalyptus*.
- Round leaves. Strong larger leaves are needed for this design – *Bergenia*, *Fatshedera* or *Hosta* are ideal.
- Round flowers.
- Spray material.

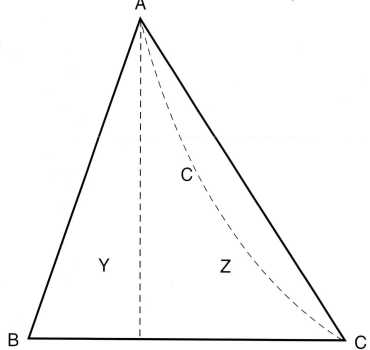

■ Asymmetric triangle.

Creating the design

1 Place the long gently-curved stem (*a*) in the top of the
  foam, two thirds of the way back and slightly to one side.
  Angle the stem so that the tip is approximately above
  where the stem enters the foam. Do not allow the stem
  tip to go beyond the centre of the foam or it will look as if
  it is falling over.

2 Place line material (*b*) one third the length of (*a*), out of the
  front of the foam angled downwards over the rim of the
  container and away from stem (*a*).

3 Place line material (*c*) half to two thirds the length of (*a*),
  out of the side of the foam and slightly forwards. You
  have now formed the triangle ABC divided by the line AD.
  Triangle ABD (area Y) will contain your heavier material
  while triangle ADC (area Z) will contain the finer material
  and incorporate more space.

4 Use larger leaves to cover the mechanics. Use them
  particularly in the narrow triangle ABD to give weight and
  strength to that side of the design. Remember that all
  stems should appear to radiate from point X. Graduate
  the size of the plant material carefully so that the design is
  a harmonious whole and does not have an arm sticking
  out ungracefully.

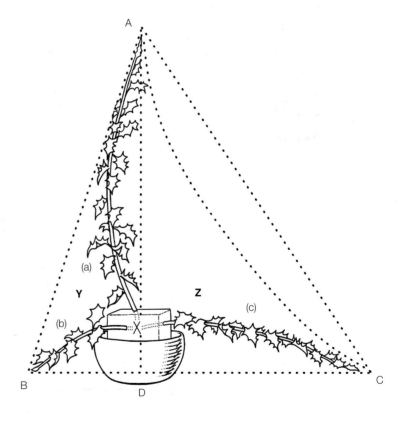

■ Next page: An asymmetric triangle created with
Leucadendron 'Safari Sunset', *Chamelaucium uncinatum*
(waxflower) together with *Lilium*, *Dianthus*, *Eustoma*
(lisianthus) and orchids. Note that the plant material on the
shorter left-hand side of the design is bolder with less space.

5 Reinforce the outline with line flowers. Do not just place them close to the boundary of the triangle but position them at different angles to build up the third dimension. Give a gentle scoop into the long side of the triangle AC to incorporate more space into the finished design.

6 Use round flowers to create the area of strongest interest. For good balance this is located around the base of the tallest stem, about two thirds of the way down. This area will therefore, be off centre.

7 Use spray material to complete the design. Do not worry if a small amount of foam is showing. This often happens at the back of the lighter side ADC. If necessary cut some filler material very short and use it to cover the gaps. Create depth and interest without destroying your shape by angling some material backwards, particularly in the deepest part of your scoop.

Variation

Use the asymmetric triangle on a tall stand with a second small design instead of an accessory.

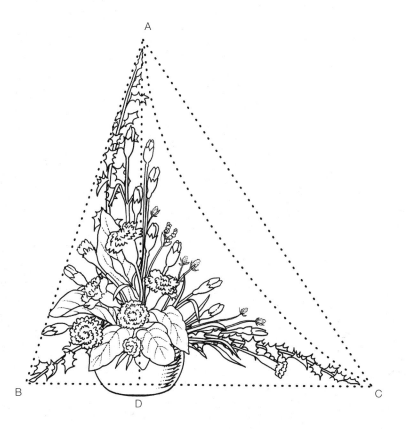

Upright circular arrangement

This circular arrangement is seen to best effect when there is an abundance of plant material available. It has a loose feel that is not contrived. It must have a raised container as extra height is needed to complete the circle.

This is a symmetrical design where the plant material on each side of the central axis will be similar but not the same. It is to be viewed all round and is therefore seen to advantage when placed centrally on a table.

You will need:

- A raised container at least 25 cm (10 in) high.
- For mechanics you can wedge foam into the opening of the container or vase or, alternatively, insert a small inner bowl into the opening.
- Foam and florists' tape. As a large amount of plant material is used the foam needs to be firmly secured within the container. A length of florists' tape can be used to keep the foam secure.
- Line foliage and flowers.
- Round or looped leaves – these need to be smooth textured.
- Round flowers.
- Spray material. ·

Creating the design

1 Place the soaked foam in the containers so that it rises approximately 4–7 cm (1.6 in–2.8 in) above the rim of the container. Insert stem (*a*) of line plant material in the centre of the foam. This stem should be the height of the container but should not include the height of the foam. When you have placed the first stem you will probably think it looks too short – don't worry it isn't.

   The line YZ is the diameter of the circle. The other placements will fill in this circle. The base of the container (Z) is completing the circle. X is not only the imaginary point from which all stems should radiate, it is also the central point of the circle.

2 Stems (*b*) are the same length as (*a*). These will be positioned in all directions out of the foam but ALL stems will appear to radiate from point X. You need to position the stems so that there is a uniform distance between the stems. Angle stems downwards over the rim of the container.

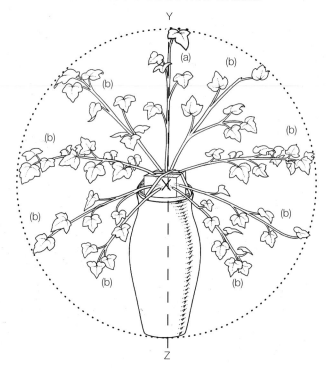

- Right: A raised round arrangement in a traditional urn. *Eucalyptus cinerea* and *Ruscus hypophyllum* form the outline with looped *Aspidistra* highlighting the mini *Gerbera*, *Rosa* sp. 'First Red', *Lysimachia* and *Eustoma*. Whole limes give interest and a smooth texture to the design.

3 Help to cover the foam and to give a contrast of texture by placing large leaves, with a smooth texture, through the design. Don't cut the stems too short, let them have movement. They can be slightly recessed to give interest but they should not go beyond the boundaries set by the linear material.

4 Ensure that you have stems at regular intervals through the design.

5 Add round flowers through the design. The stems should be approximately the same length and placed at angles to give interest. The stems will be slightly shorter than the foliage framework.

6 Complete with sprays of berries or flowers. You may also wish to use line flowers if you have these available or perhaps some interesting foliage. You could add fruits such as lemons, apples, kiwi fruit or vegetables such as shallots or broccoli. These can be impaled on lengths of garden or kebab sticks.

Variation

Fill a tall glass container with fruit and/or vegetables. Place a shallow dish in the opening. Use similar fruit and vegetables with your flowers.

The Hogarth Curve

The Hogarth curve is attributed to the famous artist of the same name who called it the 'Line of Beauty'. It loosely follows the shape of the letter 'S'. It is a stylized shape that most people either love or hate. Creating a successful Hogarth curve gives the arranger a keen sense of achievement. It is a building block in the understanding of the use of plant material and has been included for this reason.

You will need:

- A tall, raised container at least 25 cm (10 in) high. If a bottle or candlestick is being used a small candlecup or a round plastic dish with a cork glued to the base will be required.
- A small amount of foam. It must not fill the candlecup as the more foam used the more plant material will be needed to hide the foam. This can detract from the smoothness of your shape. It must rise well above the rim. This design can also be successfully created on a pinholder.
- Curved line material. This is essential. Blossom is ideal as it takes the colour through to the limits of the design.
- Round leaves.
- Round flowers.
- Spray plant material.

Creating the design

1 The first placement (a) must be curved plant material. It should be about one and a half times the height of the container and positioned in the middle of the foam two thirds of the way back. It should be upright or angled very slightly backwards. It must not lean forwards. The tip of this stem must have an imaginary line to the centre of the foam. It must not cross over. This will not work unless the plant material has a strong curve.

2 The second stem of curved material (b) is approximately one third to one half the length of (a). It is positioned to come forward towards the viewer. It should appear to be

a natural extension of (a). The stem end is inserted in the side of the foam, or the front, so that it comes forward to create an informal 'S' shape, together with placement (a). This would give the dotted line YZ on the diagram opposite. Each stem must therefore appear to come from the imaginary point 'X' as in the other designs.

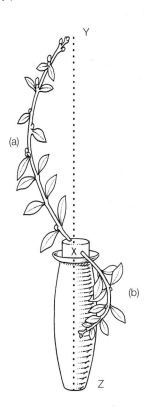

3 Position round leaves to cover some of the foam. Take care not to detract from your 'S' shape.

4 Line flowers may be added to reinforce the foliage line and to take colour through. Ensure that they are shorter than the foliage and that they follow the shape.

5 Place a round flower at the base of your tallest stem (a). Other round flowers can be used to graduate the shape carefully towards the extremities but these should be smaller or angled so that they are less dominant. Remember that one flower of a different variety or colour stands out too vividly and stops the design being seen as a whole.

6 Cover any visible foam with short lengths of spray plant material. Use the minimum amount possible. Do remember that you will be far more conscious of foam showing than anyone else. It is better to have space in your design and be able to see the form of all your components than to have it overfilled.

Fill out your shape. Think of the overall shape with every placement you make. Do not use any material that is going to obscure the shape of the 'S' in any way. You will now be thankful that you used the minimum amount of foam.

Variation

- Try a Hogarth with a wider 'S' shape.

■ *Anthurium andreanum* 'Fantasia' give impact and focal interest to this Hogarth design.

■ *Aspidistra elatior* and *Typha* leaves are coiled round *Solidaster* and *Phlox paniculata* 'Van Gogh'.

6

Contemporary design

Contemporary design has progressed with leaps and bounds from the 1960s when the 'modern' and 'abstract' designs were *de rigeur*. The United Kingdom has, to a great extent, created a contemporary style of its own. This is due to our increased awareness and application of what is happening in the flower world in Europe and beyond, combined with the availability of exotic and new plant material from all the corners of the world.

Characteristics

Some or all of the following may be evident:

- Plant material is grouped rather than scattered.
- Layering is a feature.
- There are many areas of strong interest.
- Balance is usually asymmetric, often influenced by Ikebana (the art of Japanese flower arranging).
- Plant material can radiate from the central area but frequently the stems have their own individual point of origin.
- Blocking of plant material. A flower or leaf is not seen individually but as part of a mass of colour and or form.
- Bold, exotic plant material such as *Strelitzia*, *Zantedeschia*, orchids and palms are used extensively.
- If a container is used it is often strong and sculptural and constitutes an essential part of the overall design.
- Colour is often bold and striking.
- The container may be more dominant or less dominant than the plant material.
- Woody structures are often incorporated into the design to give depth and interest.
- Accessories such as fabric, glass and decorative coloured wire are used to give interest.
- Leaves are manipulated to change their form to give excitement, space and volume. A flat leaf is very 2D. The third dimension is brought into play when woven, plaited, curled or twisted. The textural surface can be changed and curiosity can be created.
- Space is not always evident within the design but space will always exist around the overall form. Space always exists within volumetric forms. Enclosed space is created by curving twigs and branches, manipulated plant material and strap leaves, tucked in at both extremities to form bridges.
- Mechanics are innovative – test tubes, constructions, rusty metal scraps and chicken wire are used in novel and interesting ways.

Techniques

The following terms and techniques are those principally used in this section that relate to contemporary design.

Massing or blocking

Massing or blocking of one type of plant material is something of a modern phenomenon. Immediate impact is achieved through a mass of colour and texture. Individual form does not exist – only the mass as a whole. Space only occurs within the design by cutting stems to different lengths within the mass to avoid flatness.

Grouping

Grouping is enjoyed both in contemporary and in classic design where it gives a contemporary edge. It is exciting and challenging but how can it be successfully achieved?

Flowers are grouped not scattered. There is often only one group placement of each variety of flower. The important criteria is balance. Each time a placement is made it must be balanced by another placement although the colour, form and texture is unlikely to be identical. In classic design there can be greater variance in the length of stems.

Bunching

Bunching is taking several or many of the same variety of flower and placing the stems together in parallel format to form one unit. The stems can then be placed freely in position or tied with raffia or similar materials which blend. The tie should be of secondary interest.

The stems can be approximately the same height or step down in height.

Bundling

Bundling is another term for the mass positioning of one variety of flowers in a parallel format. The difference is that the tie is of decorative interest, for example coloured wire, and an integral part of the design.

Groundwork/Patchwork/Tuft work/ Carpeting/Paving

This is when the base of a design is covered with very short stems of plant material of varying forms, colours and textures. One type of plant material leads into another which distinguishes itself by virtue of strong contrast. There can be some variation in height.

Layering or terracing

A way of understanding layering is to think of tiles on a roof. Layering can be:

■ The placing of several or many of the same type of leaf on top of each other. They can be slightly angled to give depth and movement.

■ Overleaf: A design showing simple grouping. *Rosa* sp. 'Leonidas', *Lilium* 'Casablanca' (lilies), *Dianthus*, limes and *Pinus* (pine cones) surround three gold candles.

■ *Tulipa* 'Van Rijn', *Eustoma grandiflorum*, *Celosia* and *Viburnum opulus* 'Roseum' balance each other through the skilful grouping of plant material with regard to colour, form and texture, unified with strards of silver thread.

■ In a cascade design layers of different types of plant material are built up, one on top of the next, to give contrast of form and texture.

For examples of bunching, bundling, groundwork and layering look at the photographs on pages 87–8.

Leaf Manipulation

Taking a leaf and changing its form is possible with tough, long-lasting plant material such as *Phormium* (New Zealand flax*)*, *Aspidistra*, Japanese aralia (*Fatsia*), *Galex urceolata*, palm, *Bergenia* and ivy. The following are some of the techniques commonly practised:

■ Two blocked forms of apples and chrysanthemums are captured by the graphic lines of *Equisetum hyemale*. Placed on a low plate the design holds rhythm.

Graphic line forms

Perhaps the best plant material that lends itself to graphic line forms is the horsetail (*Equisetum*). Its straight form can be easily manipulated at angles, thus giving space within an arrangement.

Twisting

Take two strong leaves such as *Aspidistra* together with upper surfaces facing each other. Staple tips then twist one leaf against the other. Tape the stems together after twisting.

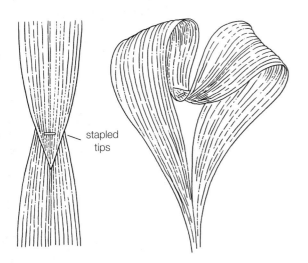

stapled tips

■ Large rolled leaves surround a mass of *Hypericum* 'Honey Flair'.

Rolling

This can be effected in two ways:

1 Take a *Galex* or *Bergenia* leaf and roll it into a cone shape (a).

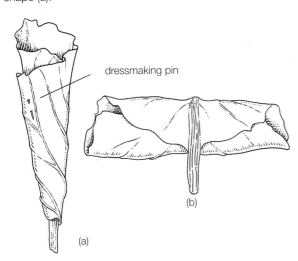

dressmaking pin

(b)

(a)

2 Roll the leaf upon itself horizontally (b). Any strong evergreen leaf can be used for this purpose. Secure with staples or dressmaking pins.

Looping

1 Push the sharp end of a leaf through the lower part of a linear leaf but make sure that you do not make the hole too large.

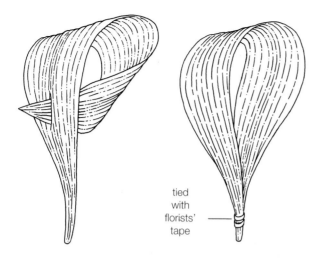

tied
with
florists'
tape

2   Loop the tip of the leaf down to meet the top of the stem
and tie with florists' tape. This technique can be seen in
the handtied on page 14.

Wiring

Place wire along the central length of a strong leaf and
secure with tape. Manipulate by coiling or bending in
places to give an undulating form

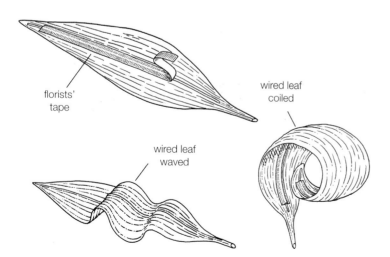

florists'
tape

wired leaf
coiled

wired leaf
waved

Plaiting

Various advanced sculptural forms can be made based
on French plaiting with palms such as Areca or Kentia.
It is easiest to learn this form of manipulation at a
workshop or day school.

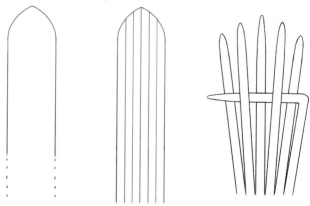

Weaving

Divide a leaf such as *Phormium* into six strips
lengthways. Weave the first strip over the second then
under the third and so on until the strip is on the

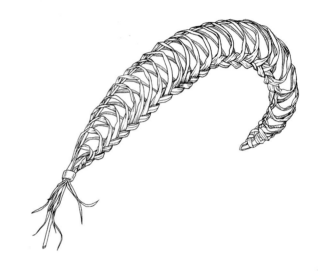

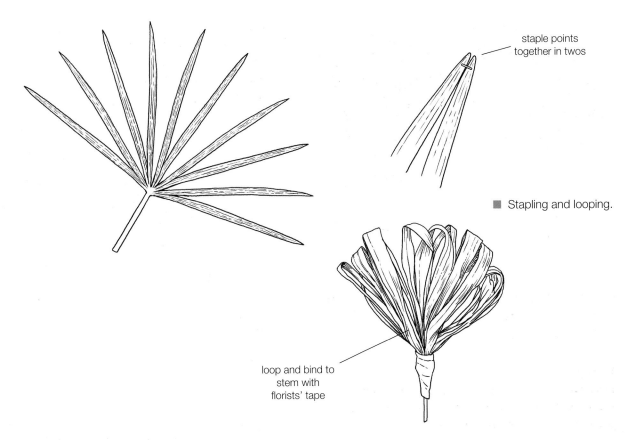

staple points
together in twos

■ Stapling and looping.

loop and bind to
stem with
florists' tape

opposite side to where you started. Repeat with the other strips until one is left. Turn the work over and repeat until one is left. Tie with wire about 5 cm (2 in) from tip end. Add to the design in loop form.

Stapling

This method of plant manipulation is ideal for small *Rhapis*, or miniature fan palms. The tips of the palms are stapled together in twos (and if there are three left at the end these three are then stapled together). The tips are then bent over and taped to the top of the stem.

Folding

Take a *Phormium* or *Cordyline* leaf and split. Bring one section across the other sections at a 90° angle. Take second section across the first. Repeat to at least 10 cm (4 in).

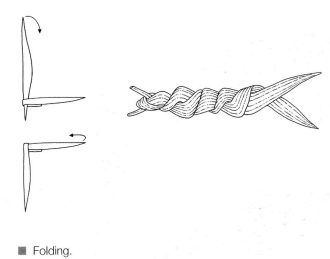

■ Folding.

Parallel style

This style became popular in Great Britain at the end of the twentieth century. The style originated in the low countries predominantly using flowers and foliage from the florist. The style has been adapted to the plant material available in British gardens, to which it is ideally suited. It often has a less structured form than that on the Continent of Europe.

Characteristics

- There is little or no radiation of plant material.
- Plant material is grouped rather than scattered.
- There is great emphasis on form and texture.
- The most frequently seen designs are created on a floral ring or posy pad or in a slim, rectangular container that is low sided in relation to the height of the completed design.
- Bare stems are an important feature of the design.
- The outline is rectangular.
- Space occurs between the groups.

- Techniques include most of those mentioned on page 79, such as grouping, bunching, bundling, groundwork and layering.

The following gives guidelines on how to create a front-facing arrangement that can be viewed from three sides.

You will need:

- A low rectangular dish.
- Foam to fill the inside of the container.
- An assortment of flowers and foliage chosen for their form and texture. Plant material with smooth or interesting stems give height. Smooth leaves are ideal for layering. You will probably need more material that you originally thought to cover your foam.
- Flat moss, reindeer moss, *Tillandsia* (Spanish moss) – all these can be used to cover the base inexpensively.
- Fruit, vegetables and/or pebbles which will give additional colour, form and texture.

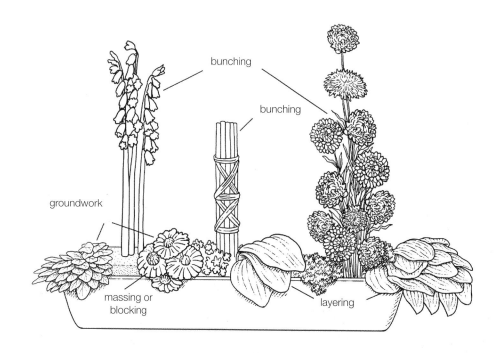

groundwork

bunching

bunching

massing or blocking

layering

Creating the design

1 Soak your foam and fill the inside of the container but slice off a corner at the rear to allow easy watering. The foam should rise sufficiently above the rim of the container so that you are able to layer the ends/sides of the design.

2 Create your vertical placements. For a container approximately 25 cm (10 in) long three verticals look the most effective. For a 30 cm (12 in) container you may need more. Avoid having the vertical placements the same height as they would look too predictable. The central placement of the three verticals is often the shortest. The verticals should **not** be positioned too close to the side edges of the container or the balance will be upset. The verticals can be bound with raffia, bunched at the same height if their stems are interesting, or simply graduated down in length (see bunching and bundling page 79). Each stem, however, will have its own point of origin and will not radiate from a central core, although minor radiation does frequently exist to give a less rigid design.

3 You will now need to cover your foam with plant material. This is kept short and is used in blocks of contrasting form, texture and colour. This is often referred to as 'ground work'. Layering is also a feature of this design. It is vital that your plant material comes over the rim of the container – particularly at the front and sides of the design. The rim should be mostly obliterated by plant material. Paths can be created through the central two thirds of the design with plant material meandering through from the front to rear. Ideally, do not use a single variety of plant material more than once.

4 Fruit on sticks, vegetables, stones and pebbles can be added into the design to heighten interest. Use the techniques that form part of this design to give an original and exciting design.

■ Previous page: A parallel design that combines *Rosa* sp., *Freesia*, *Dianthus*, *Cotinus coggygria*, *Cordyline australis*, *Parthenocissus quinquefolia*, *Corylus avellana* 'Contorta', *Bixia orellana*, variegated *Hosta* and *Bergenia* leaves with the fruit of the *Kiwano*.

■ *Molucella laevis* (bells of Ireland), *Scabiosa* seedheads and larkspur create the verticals in this parallel design. The groundwork is composed of *Tellima* leaves and individual ivy leaves. Roses and smooth pebbles create low areas of strong interest.

Cascade

Does the cascade or waterfall, as it is sometimes called, come under the heading of classsic or contemporary design? It bears characteristics of both. The plant material radiates from a central core but layering is very much a feature. The style is said to be based on a traditional shower wedding bouquet. It could also be viewed as an extension of a downward crescent. It is, therefore, with a certain amount of confidence but not total conviction that it is included in this section.

You will need:

- A tall stand, such as a pedestal metal stand, candle stick or plinth.
- A piece of foam.
- A piece of 1.25 cm (½ in) chicken wire.
- Some large leaves and mixed foliage such as *Bergenia*, large *Fatsia*.
- Long flowing sprays of foliage such as soft ruscus, (*Danae racemosa*), *Eucalyptus*.
- Several bold long leaves such as *Phormium tenax*, *Aspidistra*.
- Linear and/or spray flowers, such as *Eustoma* (lisianthus), small-headed roses or small callas (*Zantedeschia*).
- Large focal flowers such as open lilies, paeonies, gerbera.

Creating the design

1   Cover the foam with chicken wire and secure with florists' tape. The foam should rise well above the rim of the container.
2   The foam should be covered so that the foam is still visible but not obvious. This is done by using some large, plain leaves together with mixed foliage to give variety.
3   Create the height, length, width and depth of the overall design. Do this by first using the long flowing plant material. The tallest stem should be placed two thirds of the way back in the length of the foam and for an overall design of 90 cm (3 ft) be about 22 cm (9 in) tall. It should be no more. It is a design that can be viewed all round.

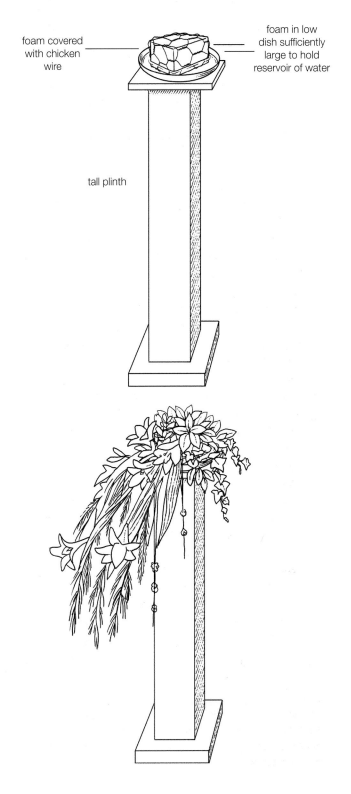

foam covered with chicken wire

foam in low dish sufficiently large to hold reservoir of water

tall plinth

■ *Danae racemosa*,
Xerophyllum tenax
(bear grass), *Lilium*
'Sisi' (lilies), *Gerbera*,
Hedera helix,
Phormium and
Chamelaucium
uncinatum
(waxflower) combine
to give a flowing
cascade design.

4　Place several long plain-textured leaves, such as
Phormium (these can be split if they are too wide) through
the long line of the design. Do, however, keep within the
boundaries set by the flowing plant material.

　　The next layer takes light-flowing flowers to take colour
to the margins of the design. The stems need to be flexible
rather than the rigid stems of say a chrysanthemum.

5　Large, bold flowers then take the stage. These are
positioned away from the perimeter of the design to give
a strong mass more centrally.

6　The next layer creates another dimension and is gentle
and light. It could be *Gypsophila*, *Limonium*, *Asparagus*
fern or slender strap leaves wrapped around the main
area of the overall design.

7　Finally you can add extra interest by introducing elements
that would give added interest, such as coloured reel wire,
a hanging element, mossed spheres or flowers linked with
garden twine, wool or wire. Individual flowers placed in
glass tubes and suspended with wire would also look good.

Structures (constructions)

Structures or constructions are made from fresh or
dried plant material, most usually with twigs or
trailing stems, secured by tying, nailing, threading,
weaving, winding, wedging or bending.

Structures, or grid forms, may be used in place of
ordinary mechanics. They can also be added to give
decorative as well as supportive value.

The plant material used for making structures may be:

- of trailing habit, e.g. climbers such as *Clematis*, ivy
  (*Hedera*), jasmine (*Jasminum*) and Boston ivy
  (*Parthenocissus*);
- of weeping habit, e.g. birch (*Betula*) and willow
  (*Salix*);
- stems or twigs of a woody nature, e.g. gum
  (*Eucalyptus*), *Kerria*, roses or stripped willow.

Lengths of either trailing or weeping habit can be
wound or tied together at random or fixed in definite
patterns to give rings or spheres. Woody stems are
used to create grids, scaffolding or wigwams.

Types of Structures

Rings (wreaths)

Rings are created by winding one length upon another.
The form can be secured by wrapped lengths of wire,
or finer stems, around at intervals to catch the rings
together. Alternatively, if the lengths are fresh you
may need only to catch ends between the circles of
plant material.

Rings with wires incorporated can form the basic
structure within which a contemporary handtied
can be created. *Clematis montana* trails or lengths of
flexible birch are ideal for making rings but you need
more than you may think initially to achieve a full and
interesting wreath or ring.

■ A ring structure has been placed on a straight sided glass
tank containing fragrant white paperwhites. Cut stems of
pussy willow are scattered around the container.

Spheres

The intersection of three rings, two at right angles and a third secured around the equator make a starting point for spheres. They can be strengthened by additional plant material and then spray painted, glittered or wound with embroidery silks or coloured reel wire. This type of sphere makes an interesting contrast to foam spheres which are decorated in various ways, as seen opposite.

Wet foam balls can be covered with:

- flat moss;
- *Galax* or laurel leaves secured with brass tacks or dressmaking pins;
- grey furry leaves to give interesting texture;
- round flowers – carnations are ideal.

Dry foam spheres can be covered with:

- cloves;
- reindeer moss;
- glycerined leaves;
- dried or preserved leaves or flowers.

Grids, scaffolding and wigwams

Woody stems can be cut into pieces of a chosen length and tied tightly with raffia, willow bark, strands of *Phormium*, paper-coated or decorative wire. Garden prunings form a good source of stems for such structures.

Grids

Grids are created by placing clean stems of equal lengths into a grid formation with roughly equal spaces between the lines on a flat surface. The grid is then secured with lengths of vine wire, garden twine, raffia or tape. Grids can be used decoratively. They can

also be an important support for other plant material as well as being decorative. A grid can be trimmed to fit inside a glass container.

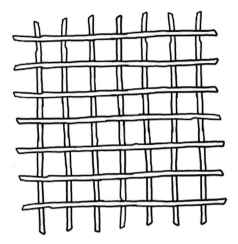

■ Stems laid on flat surface in a grid formation.

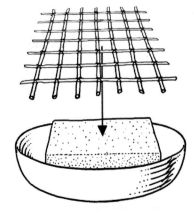

■ Secured grid placed over foam.

■ Left: A mass of complimentary spheres created from *Dianthus*, flat moss wrapped with gold bouillon wire, overlapping *Elaegnus* leaves secured with pins, *Galax urceolata* pinned, *Solidago* cut very short, and clove balls decorated with raffia.

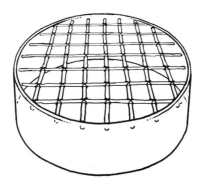

■ Grid trimmed to fit interior of bowl using a straight-sided container.

Scaffolding

Perhaps the simplest form of scaffolding is to create a square of four equal lengths of plant material. Four longer, equal lengths of the same plant material are then added at right angles, the ends of which are inserted into foam to create an upright structure.

■ A scaffolding structure created with the straight stems of *Equisetum hyemale* and secured with raffia ties. *Oncidium*, *Cyperus involucratus*, *Gloriosa superba* 'Rothscildiana', *Zantedeschia* 'Black Magic' and *Heliconia* have been added to the design.

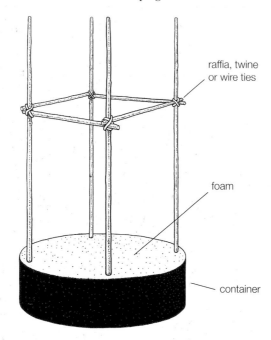

raffia, twine or wire ties

foam

container

■ Scaffolding.

■ A structure in a glass bowl with a trimmed grid of stems forms the basic structure through which vertical stems of stripped *Foeniculem vulgare* (fennel) have been inserted to create a secondary structure. *Alocasia* x *amazonica* leaves 'callas' and red roses have been added to give excitement and focal interest.

Wigwams or Obelisks

One of the simplest kinds of structures is a wigwam where three rods made from straight twigs or thin canes are put singly into foam at points around the edge of a straight-sided container. The rods are tied tightly at a selected distance from their free ends so that a tapering pyramidal shape is formed. This basic geometric form can be embellished by the addition of horizontal or oblique cross pieces and by winding or threading linear leaves such as bear grass, *Iris* or *Phormium* leaves through.

A free-standing structure suitable for use with or without floral foam can also be prepared by using long stems together with two smaller concentric triangles of bound smaller stems – one wedged in the middle of the pyramid and held in place by enclosing the larger stem triangle towards the pyramid's base. One or more small plant saucers to hold foam can be supported and secured within the structure by the addition of cross pieces as required. The inclusion of coiling lengths of trailing plant material, such as ivy, gives rhythm to the rather static geometric wigwam form.

Where larger structures are desired or shapes which would be unable to stand on their own, additional support may be added incorporating a metal stand with a heavy base. This may be spray or brush painted in colours which tone with the structure or camouflaged with string, hessian, sisal fibre, flat moss, grass or similar or lichen fungi, bark or overlapping leaves.

■ A wigwam on a ring base secured with decorative wire, *Hedera helix* drapes the structure and *Helianthus annuus* are positioned within the structure to give focal interest.

Graphic line forms

Hollow stems like snake grass (*Equisetum hyemale*) can be bent to give graphic line forms which can be secured with short dressmaking pins or simply inserted into foam.

Curving forms

Flexible stems such as willow withies or dogwood can be manipulated or bent and fixed to form curving structures. These can be used as frameworks in hand-tied arrangements or perhaps hung with flowers in crystal test tubes or in plastic orchid tubes covered with long-lasting leaves or fabric.

Modern mass designs

The modern mass design is a glorious juxtapositioning of colour, form and texture. It is a delight to create. The space in the design appears through the bridging of plant material such as plaited palms, driftwood and so on and is subtle but dynamic. The cost of creating modern mass arrangements can be high but it is easy to incorporate elements such as pebbles, balls of wool, fruit and vegetables. This can also make design fun and eclectic.

■ Previous page: Curving forms created with stripped *Salix* (willow) canes and decorated with tulips in glass test tubes tied with electricians' rachet closures. The sphere has been covered with tulip bulbs and leaf strips.

■ A horizontal mass design of *Cymbidium* orchids featuring manipulated palm leaves (see page 84).

■ A vertical mass arrangement of *Heliconia* sp., *Anthurium andreanum* 'Choco', *Anthurium andreanum* var., *Dahlia*, apple, pink fabric, black leather and *Celosia* 'Bombay Pink'.

■ A vertical mass landscape. Circles of foam bound with grasses *Panicum virgatum*, *Xanthorrhea australis* (steel grass) and decorated with *Craspedia globosa*, *Rosa* sp. 'Leonidas', *Anigozanthos* (kangaroo paw) and *Hypericum* 'Excellent' berries.

■ Umbrella fern shelters a curving design composed of *Amaranthus*, *Gloriosa*, *Acacia*, and trailing *Asparagus* fern.

■ A circular mass design is a tapestry of *Dendrobium* orchids, *Aranthera* 'Ann Black', *Leucospermum cordifolium* (pincushion protea), sp., *Berzelia squarrosa*, cones, shredded *Aspidistra* leaves, driftwood, Ivy fabric, *Dianthus* and *Nephrolepsis exaltata*.

The movement of the design can be:

- circular;
- horizontal;
- vertical;
- curvilinear;

All designs have the following in common:

- The designs can be seen as a rich tapestry of colour, form and texture.
- Enclosed space is created with bridging material and manipulated leaves.
- Decorative detailing can be given with beads, coloured wire, wool and fabric.
- Bold and delicate plant material can be used in the same design but the greater need is for strong forms.
- Design can be formal or more informal.
- Foam is frequently used as mechanics.
- Often there is no visible container as part of the design.
- Colours are generally strong and vibrant.

Creating the design

1 Soak the posy pad briefly.
2 To create the design you need to group your plant material. Each group should be placed against another which contrasts in form and texture. Rather than working from one side to another balance each group with another so that each group is positioned the design as a whole is balanced.
3 A larger design can be created by extending the outline with more linear plant material.
4 Add leaves, fruit or fabric with a smooth, plain texture to give calm relief.
5 Interest is created by gently varying the height of the individual elements that are grouped together. Only a limited amount of space, however, is incorporated.
6 Include elements using the layering technique. The finished effect will be a tapestry of colour, form and texture.
7 Add bridges formed from undulating small pieces of driftwood or twigs to give rhythm, enclose space, and supply further interest.

Circular modern mass design

You will need:

- a posy pad.
- 10–15 different groups of items.

Guidelines

- You can include organic and/or non organic items.
- Your items will need to be grouped to give impact.
- Some of the plant material needs to have a bold form.
- Try to build pathways for the eye to follow through the design.
- Although this is a low arrangement vary the heights of the plant material to give interest.
- Use flat, reindeer or *Tillandsia* (Spanish moss) to help cover the foam surface and reduce cost.

Layer design

The layer design originated in Italy in the early 1990s by Rosnella Cajello Fazio. This was the beginning of a new line which is still as popular today. The idea is to create a design using layers, whether horizontal, vertical or oblique. There are no strict rules to follow and various flowers, foliage, fruit and vegetables can be used.

For horizontal and vertical placements linear leaves such as (*Phormium*), and *Iris* are useful. You will also need bold flowers with a strong form such as (*Gerbera*), (*Anthurium*) and calla (*Zantedeschia*).

Interest is created by the juxtapositioning of different textures – rough, smooth, shiny and dull – forms and colours.

Containers

Choose a tall container with a strong sculptural shape for your first designs. A straight-sided container that is slightly wider at the top than the bottom works well as does a strong rounded container without indentations. As the container is an important part of the design the texture and colour must harmonize with the plant material. In the photograph of the design by Carla Barbaglia (page 91) she has used a classic shell container. The caption explains why it works so well.

Mechanics

Foam is the most usual means of supporting the plant material. If using a straight-sided pot the lower part of the container can be filled with foam oddments or even dry foam. Do not oversoak the foam.

- As the stems are placed in a horizontal and/or vertical direction out of the foam the foam must rise well above the rim of the container.
- Metal grids, manufactured by Flora Mec, are often incorporated into metal stands so that downward movement is easily introduced.
- Chicken wire is often wrapped round the piece of foam to make a cage and give additional support.
- Kebab, dowelling, moss pins or specialist plastic sticks can be glued at right angles to lengths of bark or wood. The sticks can be inserted into the foam.

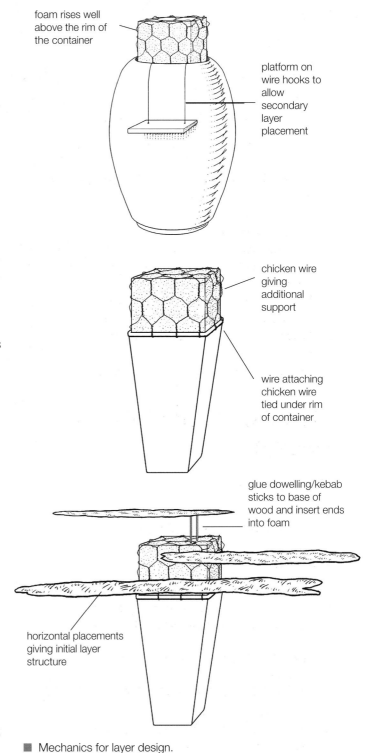

foam rises well above the rim of the container

platform on wire hooks to allow secondary layer placement

chicken wire giving additional support

wire attaching chicken wire tied under rim of container

glue dowelling/kebab sticks to base of wood and insert ends into foam

horizontal placements giving initial layer structure

■ Mechanics for layer design.

The plant material

The parallel horizontal placements are best created with natural plant material such as *Eucalyptus* bark, straight-sided pieces of *Cornus*, *Equisetum*, long cinnamon sticks, pampas grass (*Cortaderia*) or *Phormium* leaves. Branches of blossom, *Angelica* stems, bundled stripped willow and slivers of driftwood can also be used.

Bold flowers provide contrast and should complement the basic structure without changing the style. *Gerbera*, bloom chrysanthemums, *Anthurium*, calla (*Zantedeschia*) all work well.

Alternatively, you could use fruit or vegetables such as lemons, sharon fruit, ornamental cabbages or even halves of red cabbage in larger designs. You could also include non plant material such as metal pieces and plexi glass.

The design

- Different kinds of flowers and foliage can be used together. Delicate flowers such as jasmine can be used with bolder plant material.
- Bold forms tend to dominate.
- Moss can be used to camouflage the foam and give added texture.
- Space and rhythm can be added by introducing repeating looped linear leaves.

Creating the design

1 Place the foam in the container so that it is about one third of the height of the container once in position.
2 Take the linear foliage or bark and build up your layers. Create depth by building out at varying lengths and at varying depths. If possible run a piece the full length of the design. To keep these in place wrap a strong wire round the centre of the bark or stem and insert the free ends in the foam or use a bradawl to make holes through the plant material and loop your wire through and into the foam. Alternatively if a length is heavy hot glue kebab sticks to the wood at right angles to insert into the foam.
3 Cover the foam with moss and/or leaves. Build up rhythm by overlapping leaves. You could use well-conditioned leaves of *Parthenocissus tricuspicata*, *Hedera*, *Ribes*, *Fatsia* or *Fatshedera*, manipulated *Cordyline* leaves or looped bear grass to give added depth.
4 Add bold flowers such as *Anthurium*, *Gerbera*, bloom chrysanthemums and other items to add interest.

■ Previous page: The design of the shell-shaped vase is repeated in the form of the wavy leaves of the *Brahea*. Its glossy texture contrasts with the dull and rough pieces of black kelp. A further contrast is evident between the spathes of *Pandanus utilis* and the cork bark which has been bleached so that the colour of the two elements is similar but the texture totally different. Other material used is *Begonia rex*, *Crassula falcata*, *Crassula hyb.*, *Furcraea foetida*, *Hedychium gardnerianum*, *Kniphofia* hyb. and *Quercus suber*.

Inspiration

■ The flowing, undulating stems of the turban flowers (*Ranunculas*) and tulips give a rhythmic arrangement in a simple glass container. The smooth-textured green leaves of the tulips add substance and complement the round forms of the flowers.

■ Anemones are happiest with their stems in water. This topiary has been created by inserting a florist's extension cone in foam and tightly packing green garden sticks around the cone to give a decorative finish.

■ Split, dried oranges provide the focus for this simple arrangement of *Azigozanthus* (kangaroo paw), *Asclepias*, *Photinia* and *Hypericum* in a straight-sided brown pot.

■ Chicken wire covers a simple basket container through which twigs have been inserted. Hypericum, huckleberry, waxflower, red Cordyline leaves and stunning Oriental lilies fill the container. Twigs of pussy willow link with the container and give overall unity to the design.

■ *Gypsophila* always looks good on its own, creating a cloud of colour and texture. The smooth stones at the base complement the flowers, subtly yet dramatically. Further contrast is given by the terracotta container and palisade of brown stems.

Taking it further

Flower Arranging Worldwide

The World Association of Flower Arrangers (WAFA) was founded in 1981. Up-to-date information may be obtained from the National Association of Flower Arranging Societies (see below under United Kingdom for contract details).

WAFA's objectives are to reinforce the bonds between the various members and to promote the exchange of information concerning floral art interests. If you are interested in flower arranging as a hobby then do get in touch at the address given for your country – they will be able to help you further your interest in flowers.

Argentina
Mrs Susana Schiaffino
Peru 630-5-20
1068 Capitol Federal
Buenos Aires
Argentina

Australia
Mrs Norma Gordon
10 Balaka Street
Rosny
Tasmania
Australia

Barbados
The Barbados Flower
Arrangement Society
P.O. Box 8
Christchurch
Barbados
West Indies

Belgium
Belgian Flower
Arrangement Society
(B.F.A.S.)
Mrs Eliane Joski
Kortrijksesteenweg 834
B-9000-Gent
Belgium
E-mail:
BFAS@belgianflower.isabel.be

Bermuda
The Garden Club of
Bermuda
P.O. Box HM 1141
Hamilton HMEX
Bermuda
Tel: 1-441-293-2865

Canada
The Registry of Garden
Clubs of Canada
c/o Royal Botanical
Gardens
P.O. Box 399
Hamilton
Ontario L8N 3H5

France
Société Nationale
d'Horticulture de France
(SNHF–Floral Art)
Madame Jacqueline
Bogrand
84 rue de Grenelle
75007 Paris
France

Hong Kong
Hong Kong Flower Club
GPO Box 11991
Hong Kong

India
Pushpa Bitan Friendship
Society
Mrs Kavita Poddar
10 Dover Park,
Calcutta 700019
India

International
International Design
Symposium Ltd
64 Churchill Road
Westwood
MA, 02090–1602
USA
E-mail: kennstep@erols.com

Ireland
IEFA
Nuala Hegarty
96 Brookwood Avenue
Dublin 5
Ireland

Italy
Instituto Italiano per la
Decoraziano Floreale per
Amatori (IIDFA)
Mrs Rosnella Cajello Fazio
P.O. Box 229
18038 San Remo
Italy
Tel/Fax: 00 39 0184
575779

Jamaica
Jamaica Panel of Judges of
Floral Art and Horticulture
P.O. Box 203
Kingston 8
Jamaica

Japan
Nipon Flower Designers
Association
4-5-6 Takanawa
Minato-ku
Tokyo 108-8585
Japan

Kenya
Kenya Floral Arrangement
Club
Mrs Veena Sagoo
P.O. Box 6670
Nairobi
Kenya

Korea
Korea International Floral
Arts and Crafts
Development Association
Flora Suok Seoh
C.P.O. Box 4078
Seoul 100-640
South Korea

Malta
The Malta Floral Club
57 Sir Luigi Camilleri
Street
Sliema
SLM 12
Malta

Mexico
Federation Mexicana de
Jardineria y Arregio Floral
Mrs Sara Lambarri
ADPO Postal 41-842
Lomas Virreyes
Mexico DF 11000

The Netherlands
Nederlandse Amateur
Bloemschik Studieklub
(NABS)
Daisy de Vries Juncker
172 Tongerenseweg
8162 PP Epe
The Netherlands

New Zealand
The Floral Society of New
Zealand (FASNZ)
Mrs Byrta Wagsraff
3/207 Ocean Road
Mount Maunganui
New Zealand

Pakistan
Karachi Floral Art Society
Mrs Shahimah Sayeed
160c block 3
P.E.G.H.S.
Karachi, 75400
Pakistan

Peru
Club de Jardines del Para
'Floralies'
av Golf Los Incas 440
Las Villas del Golfo 11
Monterrico Surco
Lima 33
Peru

Russia
International Creative
Association of Flower
Arrangement Clubs, 'Artflora'
Mrs Nina A. Lozovaya
Gen. Ermolov str 12,28
Moscow 121293

Republic of South Africa
South Africa Flower Union
P.O. Box 1
Philloppolis 9970
Free State

South Africa
South African Floral
Institute (SAFU)
Kim Zimmerman
SAFU Secretary
33 Cyprus Road
Somerset West
South Africa 7130
E-mail: alanz@synapp.co

Switzerland
The Swiss Association of
Flower Arrangers
Mrs Susan Hafner
88 Chemin de Ruth
1223 Cologny-Geneve 2
E-mail:
lhafner@worldcom.ch

United States of America
The Garden Club of
America
14 East 60th Street
3rd Floor
New York, NY 10022
E-mail: hq@gcamerica.org

United Kingdom
National Association of
Flower Arrangement
Societies (NAFAS)
Osborne House
12 Devonshire Square
London EC2M 4FE
Tel: 00 44 207 247 5567
Fax: 00 44 207 247 7232
E-mail:
flowers@nafas.org.uk
Website: www.nafas.org.uk

Uruguay
The Garden Clubs of
Uruguay
Audrey T. Gonzalez
Rambla Tomas Berreta
6725
Monte Video
C.P. 11500
Uruguay 11500
E-mail:
audrey@chasque.apc.org

Zimbabwe
National Association of
Garden Clubs of Zimbabwe
Ms Patricia West
173 Dandro village
Emerald Hill
Harare
E-mail:
johnmus@icon.co.zw

International Flower Schools

Belgium
Daniel Ost
O-L-Vrouwplein 26
Sint Niklaas 9100
Tel: 00 32 3776 1715
Fax: 00 32 3778 1358

Czech Republic
Stredni Zahradnicka Skola
Poabi 471 CZ-276 87
Melnik

France
Guy Martin
Centre International de
Formation d'Art Floral
6 rue de la Republique
60810 Villers Saint
Frambourg
Tel: 00 33 3 44 54 43 51
Fax: 00 33 3 44 54 44 85

Monique Gautier
École Française de
Decoration Florale
8 rue du General Bertrand
75007 Paris
Tel: 00 33 1 349652
Fax: 00 33 1 40 563872
E-mail: efdf@libertysurf.fr

Germany
Gregor Lersch
Telegraphenstrasse 9
Postfach 100738
D-5483
Bad Neuenahr
Tel: 00 49 2641 7047
Groups Only

Greece
Angeliki Kokkinoy
15 AG Konstantinou Str.
18532 Piraeus
Tel: 00 30 14170282
Fax: 00 30 14125443

Hong Kong
Tonie Yuen
Unit 12B
Hua Chiao Commercial
Centre
678 Nathan Road
Kowloon
Hong Kong
Tel: 852 2395 3599
Fax: 852 2395 3590
E-mail:
tonie@tonieyuen.com.hk

Italy
I.I.D.F.A.
P.O. Box 229
18038 San Remo
Tel/Fax: 00 39 0184575779

Japan
Manako Flower Academy
Roppongi City Building 2F
3-1-25 Roppongi
Minato-ku
Tokyo 106-0082
Tel: 00 81 3 5563 7844
Fax: 00 81 3 5563 7845
E-mail: manako@big.or.jp
Website:
www12.big.or.jp/-manako

Yutaka Jimbo
Ohya Building 302
2-9-3 Kyonan-cho
Masashino-City
Tokyo 180-0023
Tel: 00 81 4223 44601

Nippon Flower Designers
Association
4-5-6 Takanawa
Minatu-ku
Tokyo 108
Tel: 00 81 3542 08741

Korea
Chun Won Lee
No. 650-21, Balsan 2 Dong
Kangsu-ku
Seoul
Tel: 00 822 2366 11710

The Netherlands
Aad Van Uffelen at Holland
College
Chrysant 1
2678 PA
De Lier, Holland
Website:
www.holland-college.nl

New Zealand
Heather Hammond
Oturu Road
RD2 Otorhanga
Waikato
Tel/Fax: 00 647 873 0824

Norway
Nils Iversen and Rolf
Torhaug
Kreativ Flora
N.Slottsgt 8
N-0517, Oslo
Tel: 00 47 22 42 2722

Spain
Luis Lopez Barreto
Escuela Andaluza de Arte
Floral
41110 Bollulos de la
Mitacion
Seville
Tel: 00 349 9557 65295

Taiwan
Susita Flower Academy
94726 Bangna Complex
Bangna Trad Road
Prakamong
Bangkok 10260

China Floral Art
Foundation
No. 6 Alley 17, Lane 111
Fu-Hsing South Road
Sec. 2, Taipei 106 R.O.C.

United Kingdom
Judith Blacklock Flower
School, Knightsbridge
4/5 Kinnerton Place South
London SW1X 8EH
Tel: 00 44 207 235 6235
Fax: 00 44 207 235 6335
E-mail:
school@judithblacklock.com
Website:
www.judithblacklock.com

Japanese Floral and Garden
Design
21 Queens Gate Place
Mews
London SW7 5DG
Tel: 00 44 207 584 7662
Website:
www.takashisawano.co.uk

Ikebana Teachers
Association
Tricia Hill
Cornhill House
The Hangers
Bishops Waltham
Hants SO32 1EF
Tel: 00 44 1489 892656

The Studio @ Montford
Cottage
Fence, Nr. Burnley
Lancs BB12 9NZ
Tel/Fax: 00 44 1282
603220
E-mail:
thestudio@montford.
p3online.net

United States of America
The American Floral Art
School
529 Wabash
Suite 610
Chicago
IL. 60605
Tel: 00 1 312 922 9328

Floral Design Institute
911 Western Avenue
Suite 575
Seattle
Washington
Tel: 00 1 206 749 9464
Fax: 00 1 206 749 9374
Email: leanne@floraldesign
institute.com
Website:
www.floralschool.com

The Flower Arranging
Study Group of the Garden
Clubs of America
Ruth Crocker
120 Avon Hill Street
Cambridge
MA 02140
USA

International Design
Symposium Ltd
64 Churchill Road
Westwood
MA 02090–1602
USA
E-mail: kennstep@erols.com

Rittners School of Floral
Design
345 Marlborough Street
Boston
MA. 02115
Tel: 00 1 617 267 3824
E-mail: stevrt@tiac.net
Website:
www.floralschool.com

This list is not, of course, exhaustive. If you would like to be mentioned in
the next edition of *Teach Yourself Flower Arranging* please contact the author at
The Judith Blacklock Flower School, Knightsbridge,
4/5 Kinnerton Place South, London SW1X 8EH.

Index

JUDITH BLACKLOCK
FLOWER SCHOOL

KNIGHTSBRIDGE

Courses in flower arranging and floristry, lasting from a half day to two weeks.

For further information contact

The Judith Blacklock Flower School, Knightsbridge.
Telephone **+44 (0) 20 7235 6235**, Fax **+44 (0) 20 7235 6335**,
E-mail: **school@judithblacklock.com**   Website: **www.judithblacklock.com**

the A-Z of teach yourself

teach yourself®

Afrikaans
Access 2002
Accounting, Basic
Alexander Technique
Algebra
Arabic
Arabic Script, Beginner's
Aromatherapy
Astronomy
Bach Flower Remedies
Beginner's Turkish
Bengali
Better Chess
Better Handwriting
Biology
Body Language
Book Keeping
Book Keeping & Accounting
Brazilian Portuguese
Bridge
Buddhism
Bulgarian
Business Studies
C++
Calculus
Cantonese
Card Games
Catalan
Chess
Chi Kung
Chinese
Chinese Script, Beginner's
Chinese, Beginner's
Christianity
Classical Music
Copywriting
Counselling
Creative Writing
Crime Fiction
Croatian
Crystal Healing
Czech
Danish
Desktop Publishing
Digital Photography
Digital Video & PC Editing
Drawing
Dream Interpretation
Dutch
Dutch Dictionary
Dutch Grammar
Dutch, Beginner's
Eastern Philosophy
ECDL
E-Commerce
Electronics

Engish Grammar as a Foreign Language
English as a Foreign Language
English for International Business
English Grammar
English Language, Life & Culture
English Verbs
English Vocabulary
English, American, as a Foreign Language
English, Correct
English, Instant, for German Speakers
English, Instant, for Italian Speakers
English, Instant, for Spanish Speakers
English, Teaching One to One
Ethics
Excel 2002
Feng Shui
Film Making
Film Studies
Finance for nn-Financial Managers
Finnish
Flexible Working
Flower Arranging
French
French Grammar
French Grammar, Quick Fix
French Language, Life & Culture
French Starter Kit
French Verbs
French Vocabulary
French, Beginner's
French, Instant
Gaelic
Gaelic Dictionary
Genetics
Geology
German
German Grammar
German Grammar, Quick Fix
German Language, Life & Culture
German Verbs
German Vocabulary
German, Beginner's
German, Instant
Go
Golf
Greek
Greek Script, Beginner's
Greek, Ancient
Greek, Beginner's
Greek, Instant
Greek, New Testament
Guitar
Gulf Arabic
Hand Reflexology
Hebrew, Biblical
Herbal Medicine
Hieroglyphics
Hindi
Hindi Script, Beginner's
Hindi, Beginner's
Hinduism
How to Win at Horse Racing
How to Win at Poker
HTML Publishing on the WWW
Human Anatomy & Physiology
Hungarian
Icelandic
Indian Head Massage
Indonesian
Internet, The
Irish

Islam
Italian
Italian Grammar
Italian Grammar, Quick Fix
Italian Language, Life & Culture
Italian Verbs
Italian Vocabulary
Italian, Beginner's
Italian, Instant
Japanese
Japanese Language, Life & Culture
Japanese Script, Beginner's
Japanese, Beginner's
Japanese, Instant
Java
Jewellery Making
Judaism
Korean
Latin
Latin American Spanish
Latin Dictionary
Latin Grammar
Latin, Beginner's
Letter Writing Skills
Linguistics
Mah Jong
Managing Stress
Marketing
Massage
Mathematics
Mathematics, Basic
Media Studies
Meditation
Mosaics
Music Theory
Needlecraft
Negotiating
Nepali
Norwegian
Origami
Panjabi
Persian, Modern
Philosophy
Philosophy of Mind
Philosophy of Religion
Philosophy of Science
Photography
Photoshop
Physics
Piano
Planets
Planning Your Wedding
Polish
Politics
Portuguese
Portuguese Grammar
Portuguese Language Life & Culture
Portuguese, Beginner's
Portuguese, Brazilian
Portuguese, Instant
Postmodernism
Pottery
Powerpoint 2002
Presenting for Professionals
Project Management
Psychology
Psychology, Applied
Quark Xpress
Quilting
Recruitment
Reflexology

Reiki
Relaxation
Retaining Staff
Romanian
Russian
Russian Grammar
Russian Language Life & Culture
Russian Script, Beginner's
Russian, Beginner's
Russian, Instant
Sanskrit
Screenwriting
Serbian
Setting up a Small Business
Shorthand, Pitman 2000
Sikhism
Spanish
Spanish Grammar
Spanish Grammar, Quick Fix
Spanish Language, Life & Culture
Spanish Starter Kit
Spanish Verbs
Spanish Vocabulary
Spanish, Beginner's
Spanish, Instant
Speaking on Special Occasions
Speed Reading
Statistical Research
Statistics
Swahili
Swahili
Swahili Dictionary
Swedish
Tagalog
Tai Chi
Tantric Sex
Teaching English as Foreign Language
Teams and Team-Working
Thai
Time Management
Tracing your Family History
Travel Writing
Trigonometry
Turkish
Typing
Ukrainian
Urdu
Urdu Script, Beginner's
Vietnamese
Volcanoes
Watercolour Painting
Weight Control through Diet and Exercise
Welsh
Welsh
Welsh Dictionary
Welsh Language Life & Culture
Wills and Probate
Wine Tasting
Winning at Job Interviews
Word 2002
World Faiths
Writing a Novel
Writing for Children
Writing Poetry
Xhosa
Yoga
Zen
Zulu